Storyboard

Mark Fletcher and Richard Munns

Contents

Introduction

Everybody loves a story! Whether it's a true story of adventure or disaster, a personal story of success or misfortune or an amusing tale of dubious integrity, stories capture the interest of the listener (or reader) and are a valuable resource in the English language classroom. The picture stories in *Storyboard* provide students with a visual springboard for various activities, which give opportunities for discussion, story-building, sequencing, vocabulary development, role play, project work and creative writing.

There are three types of story or 'genres' in *Storyboard*: human interest, reportage and comedy. Human interest stories (such as *Gap year* and *Mother Theresa*) present interesting 'true life' stories about ordinary and extra-ordinary people. Reportage stories (such as *Earthquake hits city* and *Iceland and Cuba*) are semi-authentic newspaper reports which link easily to genuine news events. Comedy stories (such as *UFO story* and *Dinner disaster*) are light-hearted stories or anecdotes which may or may not be entirely true! All of the stories are interesting in themselves and stimulate discussion. The related activities give plenty of language input and opportunities for controlled and freer practice.

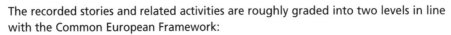

Each story consists of a page of storyboard pictures and a page of accompanying activities. There is also a page of scripts relating to each story at the back of the book. This page transcribes a recorded version of the story and an interview. (The CD track numbers are marked on the activity page.)

The recorded stories and related activities are roughly graded into two levels in line with the Common European Framework:

Stories 1–12 are pre-intermediate level

Stories 13–24 are intermediate level

However, the receptive versus productive language input can be determined to a certain extent by the teacher's exploitation of the materials. (You might, for example, choose not to focus on the higher-level language presented in the scripts.)

Suggested approach

The storyboard page

- Photocopy the storyboard pictures and the accompanying page of activities for the chosen story. (NB When using stories that include a missing picture element, make sure you hand out the activity page later as this includes the missing picture and will spoil the prediction activity.)

- Do some context setting to introduce the subject. If you've chosen 'Olympic success story' because of a current sporting event, for example, begin with a class discussion about the real event.

- The material is ideal for pair or small group work. First, read the introductory sentence in Activity 1 to set the scene. Students then go through the pictures in Activity 1 in their groups, working together to build up the story by sharing their knowledge and ideas. They can use the key words at the bottom of the page to help them. (The numbers in brackets refer to the specific frames in the story.) Some stories have a missing picture element. In these cases, the students should discuss or draw their ideas for the missing picture.

The activity page

- Activity 2 is a story-build activity consisting of a sentence per picture to be completed or put in order by the students. Once completed, Activity 2 provides them with a simple version of the story. The activities include gap-fill sentences, sentence ordering, matching sentence halves and correcting sentences. The missing picture is included on this page where relevant. Students can refer to this and compare it with their own versions of the missing picture.

- Students can then listen to a recorded version of the story in Activity 3. This version of the story expands on the simple version and provides some more detail and extra information. They can use this version to check their answers to activity 2. It is not essential that students understand every word in this full version, but there is a photocopiable script at the back of the book if they wish to read the text while they listen to the story again. (This script can also be cut up and used for story sequencing and other activities.)

- Activity 4 focuses on vocabulary in the recorded version of the story. These vocabulary-based activities include matching words to definitions, matching sentence halves and finding words in the story. Once they have completed activities 1–4, students should have all the language they need to enable them to retell the story.

- In Activity 5, students listen to an interview related to the story. These interviews either add information or throw a different light on the story and provide an interesting starting point for discussion. There are a few questions on the page to focus students' attention while listening. The recordings are semi-authentic and students are not expected to understand every word. However, the interview scripts are also included at the back of the book if they wish to study them in any detail or use them for role-play activities.

  Students are then asked to prepare their own interviews. This is a communicative exercise, which transforms narrative into dialogue. Allow a reasonable time (say ten minutes) for students to prepare their conversations, then listen to several of them. Encourage the students to visualise and dramatise their interviews.

Extension activities

- The first extension activity encourages the students to relate the story to the real world and to discuss personal opinions and experiences. They can do this as a class discussion or in groups. Having worked on the picture story in a fairly controlled way, and then listened to the interviews, the students should have plenty of linguistic material available to enable them to express their own opinions on the discussion topic. The second extension activity invites them to re-tell the story in their own words. This can be an oral or written exercise.

Extra activty

- The Extra activity is freer development emerging from the topic. Most of the suggested activities are team tasks, which will involve some brainstorming and the production of a list of ideas, a picture or an advertisement for comparison with other groups. This can lead on to further project work.

  Of course, this procedure is only one approach to the material. You might, for example, cut up the story frames for sequencing activities, and use the recorded story at the start of the lesson. Equally, the interview could be done after the extension activities. You might choose not to focus on the language in the recorded version and miss out activity 4. Similarly, you could omit one of the Extension activities depending on available time. However you choose to approach the materials, the key thing is that students should enjoy their Storyboard lesson, have opportunities to be creative in their interpretation of the images and be free to express their own opinions in the discussion phases of the lesson.

1 Another day, another dollar

1 James Cash is a very rich man. But does he have a good life?
Look at the pictures and tell the story

Here are some words to help you

servants (2)   chauffeur (3)   meetings (4)   to entertain clients (6)   to be exhausted (8)

2 Make a sentence about each picture and retell the story.
Use these words in the box to help.

1 Every morning, James has .... in bed.

2 His .... help him get dressed. He always wears a ....

3 His .... drives him to the office.

4 In the morning he has business ....

5 In the afternoon he looks at the ....

6 In the evening he .... clients.

7 At .... in the morning his chauffeur drives him home.

8 James is always ....

9 The next day is exactly the ....

> sales reports
> same
> breakfast
> chauffeur
> servants
> suit
> two o'clock
> entertains
> exhausted
> meetings

3 (1) Listen to the story and check your answers to Exercise 2.

4 Join the two halves to make full sentences.

1 James is a multi-millionaire	a because business is good.
2 He is the chairman	b to work at 7 am.
3 For breakfast he has	c and he lives in a mansion.
4 His chauffeur drives him	d at half past two.
5 Sales go up every year	e and watch a cabaret.
6 In the evenings	f boiled eggs and champagne.
7 They have dinner	g he takes clients to a night club.
8 He goes to bed	h of a big company.

5 (2) Listen to the interview with James' Personal Assistant.

a Answer the questions:
   1 Does James usually work seven days a week?
   2 Does he ever have a holiday?
   3 Does his PA like her job?

b Work in pairs and prepare an interview with James' chauffeur.
Student A is the interviewer and Student B is the chauffeur.
Ask questions like …

'What time do you start work in the morning?'
'Do you enjoy your job?'

Extension activities

a To talk about
1 How many hours a week do most people work?
2 Do most people work too hard?
3 Is it better to have longer holidays and less money?

b Write 'Another day, another dollar' in your own words.

Extra activity
– Life style

In small groups, make a list of four things that you think are good and four things you think are bad about James Cash's life. Do you think James is happy? Discuss your ideas with other groups.

2 Environmental disaster

1 Many beaches in the Philippines are covered in oil from a damaged oil tanker. Look at the pictures and tell the story.

..: *Here are some words to help you* ....

stormy weather (2)   life raft (4)   rescue boat (6)   to spray chemicals (10)   polluted (11)

2 Put these sentences in order to retell the story.

Did you guess the missing picture?

a   The fishing boat sank, but the crew got into a life raft. ☐

b   The fishermen were very cold ☐

c   The beaches are very polluted. ☐

d   In the morning a helicopter saw all the oil on the sea. ☐

e   They rescued the fishermen. ☐

f   Last night there was an accident in the South China Sea, near the Philippines. ☐ 1

g   At half past two in the morning, an oil tanker hit a fishing boat in stormy weather. ☐

h   A rescue boat went to find them. ☐

i   There was a hole in the oil tanker and tons of oil came out. ☐

j   The fishermen sent rockets from the life raft ☐

k   A lot of fish and seabirds are caught in the oil. ☐

l   Special boats are spraying chemicals on the oil. ☐

3 ◖3◗ Listen to the story and check your answers to Exercise 2.

4 Match these words to their definitions.

1 crew   a to cover with small drops of liquid

2 flare   b a crash between two things

3 to rescue   c a rocket giving bright light in the sky

4 polluted   d to pour very slowly from a hole

5 tourism   e the workers on a boat

6 bow   f the holiday industry

7 to sink   g dirty and unsafe

8 to spray   h to go to the bottom of the water

9 collision   i the front of a boat

10 to leak   j to help someone in danger

Extra activity
– Save our planet!

In small groups, list ten ways in which ordinary people can help to protect the environment. Compare your ideas with other groups.

5 ◖4◗ Listen to the interview with a fisherman.

a **Answer the questions:**
   1 Did the fishermen see the tanker before it hit them?
   2 Does the fisherman think the tanker saw them?
   3 Why is he worried?

b **Work in pairs and prepare an interview with the oil tanker captain. Student A is the interviewer and Student B is the Captain.**
   Ask questions like …
   'Where were you at the time of the collision?'
   'What did you do when you found oil was leaking?'

⋯ Extension activities ⋯⋯⋯

a   To talk about
    1 Which areas of the environment are becoming more polluted?
    2 Are any areas becoming less polluted?

b   Write 'Environmental disaster' in your own words.

3 Gap year

1 In June last year, eighteen year old Francis Thumber bought a 'World Traveller' ticket and set off on the adventure of a life time. Look at the pictures and tell the story.

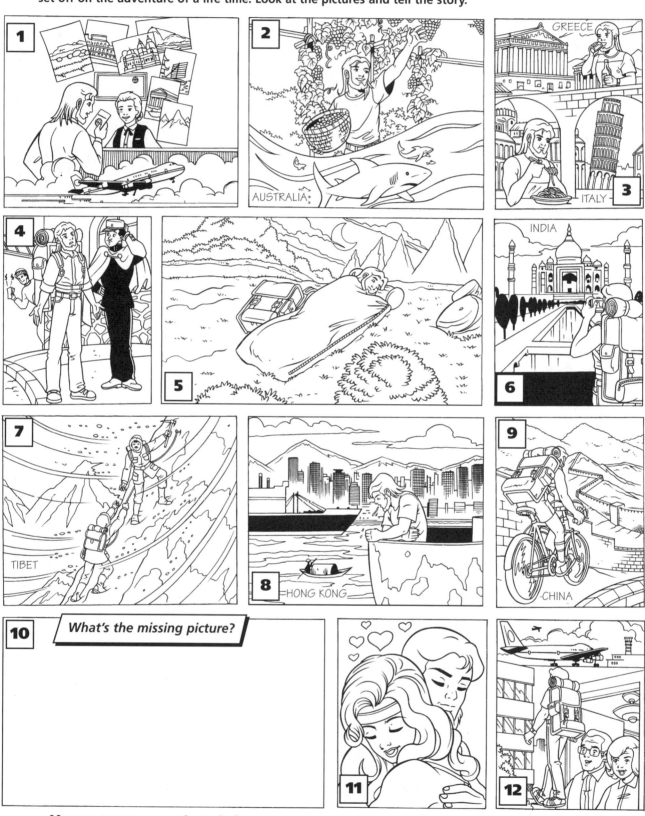

.. *Here are some words to help you* ....

to pick grapes (1) temples (3) thief (4) seasick (7) carnival (10)

2 Correct the sentences about each picture to retell the story. Use these words to help.

cycled
carnival
outside
pasta
photos
boat
~~world~~
parents
danced
mountains
sharks
money

1 Francis bought a "World Traveller" ticket and travelled around the ~~country~~ *world*.

2 He picked grapes in Australia and swam with dolphins.

3 He saw old temples in Greece and ate sausages in Italy.

4 A thief stole his clothes.

5 He had to sleep inside under the stars.

6 He took lots of trains in India.

7 He climbed trees in Tibet.

8 He went from Hong Kong to China by plane and was seasick.

9 In China he walked to the Great Wall.

10 In Rio he went to the zoo.

11 He met a beautiful girl and they worked all night.

12 He arrived home this morning and went to see his friends.

3 ⌇5⌇ Listen to the story and check your answers to Exercise 2.

4 Write the past tenses, then join the two halves to make full sentences.

1 He (climb) ...*climbed*......   **a** with sharks in Australia.

2 He (arrive) ....   **b** high mountains in Tibet.

3 He (eat) ....   **c** a 'world traveller' ticket.

4 He (cycle) ....   **d** all night in Rio.

5 He (swim) ....   **e** a lot of pasta in Italy.

6 He (visit) ....   **f** home this morning.

7 He (buy) ....   **g** Rio at Carnival time.

8 He (dance) ....   **h** to the Great Wall in China.

5 ⌇6⌇ Listen to the interview with a lifeguard.

a Answer the questions:
   1 What did the lifeguard do when he saw a shark?
   2 What does he think of Francis?

b Work in pairs and prepare an interview with Francis's mum. Student A is the interviewer and Student B is his mother.

Ask questions like …

'Where did you go?'
'What did you see / eat / do in …?'

Did you guess the missing picture?

RIO DE JANEIRO

Extra activity
– Packing

You are going on a 'Gap year'. In small groups, make a list of the 20 most important items to take with you in your rucksack.

Check your list with another group. Did you forget anything? Could you carry it all?

····· Extension activities ·········

a To talk about
Which countries would you like to visit – and why?

b Write 'Gap year' in your own words.

4 UFO story

1 Postman Joe Green spends every night in a field waiting for another visit 'from outer space'. Look at the pictures and tell the story.

.. *Here are some words to help you* ....

UFO (2) to land (3) to take off (5) control panels (6) to laugh at (10)

2 Join the two halves to make full sentences and retell the story.

1 Joe Green is   a in a field near his house.

2 One evening he saw   b took off.

3 It landed   c around the earth.

4 He climbed   d a postman.

5 The UFO   e in the same field.

6 Joe looked at   f told his wife.

7 The UFO flew   g police station and told the duty officer.

8 It landed   h a UFO in the sky.

9 He went home and   i his friends laughed at his story.

10 He went to the   j inside the UFO.

11 At the pub   k he goes to the field and waits there.

12 Every night   l the control panels.

3 (7) Listen to the story and check your answers to Exercise 2.

4 Match these words to their definitions.

1 alien   a to go around

2 glowing   b a creature from another planet

3 flight deck   c to come back

4 to orbit   d shining with light

5 to reappear   e interested

6 to land   f to fly up into the sky

7 curious   g to touch down on the ground

8 to take off   h the room where the flying controls are

5 (8) Listen to the interview with Joe's wife.

a Answer the questions:
   1 Does Joe's wife believe in UFOs?
   2 What does she think happened that night?

b Work in pairs and prepare an interview with an alien on the UFO.
   Student A is the interviewer and Student B is the alien.

Ask questions like …
'Where do you come from?'
'How long did your trip take?'

Extension activities

a To talk about
   There have been many reports of UFOs. Do you think there are
   visitors from space?

b Write 'UFO story' in your own words.

Extra activity
– The visitor

Draw your own creature from
another planet.
Do not let your partner see
your creature! Now describe
it to your partner who must
draw it. Compare
your pictures.

5 Football crazy

1 Do you like football …? Look at these pictures and tell the story

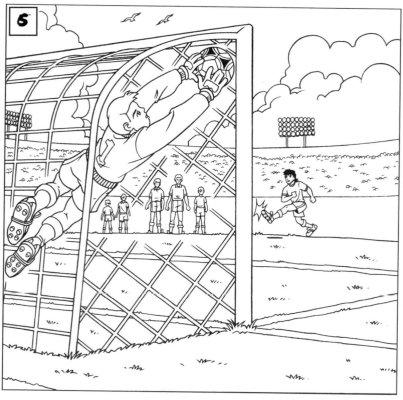

.. Here are some words to help you ....

stadium (2) to score (4) foul (5) to save (6) highlights (9)

2 Make a sentence about each picture and retell the story. Use these words to help.

1   Jim and his dad decided to go to a football ....

2   They got to the .... at ten to three.

3   The .... came onto the .... and the game started.

4   Liverpool scored the first goal and the .... cheered.

5   In the second half there was a .... by a Liverpool player and the

    .... gave a penalty to Munich.

6   The Liverpool goalkeeper saved the ....

7   Liverpool .... the game one-nil.

8   When they got home, Jim's mum was in the ....

9   Jim and his dad took their supper into the sitting room and watched the

    .... of the game on TV.

> players
> foul
> referee
> kitchen
> stadium
> crowd
> highlights
> pitch
> penalty
> won
> match

3 (9) Listen to the story and check your answers to Exercise 2.

4 Join the two halves to make full sentences.

1 They arrived at the stadium   a a penalty to Munich.
2 Liverpool scored a goal   b at twenty-five past three.
3 There was a foul   c at half past six.
4 The referee gave   d by a Liverpool defender.
5 The goalkeeper   e at ten to three.
6 The Munich supporters were   f on a tray.
7 Jim and his dad got home   g disappointed.
8 They put their supper   h annoyed.
9 Jim's mum was   i saved the penalty.

5 (10) Listen to the interview with a Munich fan.

a   Answer the questions:
    1 Is the fan happy with the referee?
    2 What was the fan going to do after the match?

b   Work in pairs and prepare an interview with Jim's mum. Student A is
    the interviewer and Student B is Jim's mum. Ask questions such as:

    'What did Jim and his dad do on Saturday?'
    'What did they do in the evening?'

Extension activities

a   To talk about
    What is the best sporting event you have ever seen?
b   Write 'Football crazy' in your own words.

Extra activity
– The match

Play this game in pairs. Each
player draws a 'goal', 7 squares
by 4 squares. In secret, each player
draws a goal keeper (5 squares)
and two defenders (two squares
each). Take turns to 'shoot' at the
goal. eg: A: D4. B: Saved by
a defender!
A: C6, B: Saved by the
goalkeeper
A: B6, B: Goal!

	1	2	3	4	5	6	7
a							
b							
c							
d							

6 Mother Teresa

1 This very special lady spent her life helping other people.
Look at the pictures and tell her story.

1 Mother Teresa born 1910 Macedonia

2

3 1929

4 Sisters of Charity

5

6 1979 · Nobel Prize for Peace

7 Today

.. *Here are some words to help you* ....

to be born (1)   a nun (2)   the poor (3)   shelters (5)   a prize (6)

2 Join the two halves to make full sentences and retell the story.

1 Mother Teresa was born   **a** continue to help the poor.

2 She became   **b** the Nobel Prize for Peace.

3 In 1929 she went to India   **c** provide shelters on the streets of the Calcutta.

4 She started an organisation   **d** a nun.

5 The Sisters run clinics and   **e** called the Sisters of Charity

6 In 1979 Mother Teresa got   **f** to work with poor people.

7 Today the Sisters of Charity   **g** in 1910 in Macedonia

3 (11) Listen to the story and check your answers to Exercise 2.

4 Match these words to their definitions.

1 homeless   **a** a child without a mother or father

2 pavement   **b** a safe place to live

3 peace   **c** a member of an all-women's religious group

4 nun   **d** without a home

5 orphan   **e** the path beside the road

6 shelter   **f** when there is no war

7 charity   **g** a group that gives money and food to people in need

5 (12) Listen to the interview with a charity worker.

a Answer the questions:
    1 What does the Charity do?
    2 How do they get their money?

b Work in pairs and prepare an interview with one of the Sisters of Charity.
    Student A is the interviewer and Student B is a Sister of Charity.
    Ask questions like …
    'Where were you born?'
    'When did you start working here?'

Extra activity
– The radio appeal

In small groups prepare (and record) a one-minute radio appeal on behalf of a charity.

Explain why the charity needs money and how the money will be used.

Extension activities

a To talk about
What other organisations do you know that give help to people in need?
Have you ever given money to a charity?
b Write 'Mother Teresa' in your own words.

7 Dinner disaster

1   Mr. Smith invited his boss, Mr. Plummer to dinner – BUT they forgot about the cat … . Look at the pictures and tell the story.

.. *Here are some words to help you* ....

> to invite (1)   a salmon (2)   to lay the table (3)   to be horrified (6)   to rush out (7)

2 Make a sentence about each picture and retell the story. Use these words to help you.

  1 Mr Smith phoned his boss and .... him and his wife to dinner.

  2 Mr and Mrs Smith .... a salmon for dinner.

  3 They .... the table with .... and bottles of wine .

  4 Mrs Smith put on an evening .... and Mr Smith wore his best suit.

  5 The Plummers .... at eight o'clock.

  6 When they saw the table, they were .... The main plate was ....

  7 Mrs Smith .... into tears and Mr Smith .... out of the house.

  8 He ran to the .... shop.

  9 They had a lovely evening, and so did the ....

> dress
> burst
> cat
> prepared
> fish and
>   chip
> empty
> horrified
> invited
> laid
> arrived
> rushed
> candles

3 (13) Listen to the story and check your answers to Exercise 2.

4 Who do you think said these words?

1 Wonderful. We'd love to come.

2 Does this dress suit me?

3 I hope this sauce will be OK!
....

4 I'll be right back!
....

....

5 We'd like to invite you to dinner this Friday.

6 It's good to see you again. Do come in.

7 The table looks beautiful.
....

....

8 Oh, no!

9 Everything was delicious. Thank you

10 Miaow!

....

....

Extra activity
– Your dinner party

In small groups plan a dinner party for an important visitor. Write the menu for four courses. Don't forget drinks!

5 (14) Listen to the interview with Mr and Mrs Plummer.

  a Answer the questions:
    1 Are the Plummers and the Smiths close friends?
    2 What are the first names of Mr and Mrs Smith?
    3 Are they going to meet again?

  b Work in pairs and prepare an interview with the cat. Student A is the interviewer and Student B is the cat. Ask questions like …
  'What is your favourite food?'
  'Do you often take food from the table?'

Extension activities

  a To talk about
     Have you ever been to a party where something went wrong?
  b Write 'Dinner disaster' in your own words.

8 Fashion fads

1 Fashions change all the time. They have changed a lot since 1860!
Look at the pictures and tell the story.

1 Victorian times

Sportswear in 1880

2

3 The 1920s

Wartime

4

The 1960s

5

6

The 1970s

7 Today

.. *Here are some words to help you* ....

formal (1) sportswear (2) uniform (4) casual (5) unisex (6)

2 Correct the sentences about each picture to retell the story. Use these words to help.

                       dresses

1   In Victorian times women wore long ~~trousers~~ and men wore heavy jackets.

2   Men wore striped shorts and caps for tennis and women wore long dresses and hats.

3   In the 1920s, the 'Flappers' wore cheap clothes.

4   During the wartime, of course, lots of people wore pyjamas.

5   In the 1960s women wore long skirts and men's clothes became more colourful.

6   Ten years later, clothes for men and women were similar. Everyone wore blue shoes!

7   Now young people wear fleeces with hoods or swimming caps and you see a lot of body piercings or tattoos.

> baseball
> uniforms
> mini
> ~~dresses~~
> jackets
> expensive
> jeans

3 (15) Listen to the story and check your answers to Exercise 2.

4 Look at the pictures in Activity 1. Write the number of the picture where you can see the following clothes. Write the period when the clothes were fashionable.

	Clothes	Picture(s)	Period
1	a full skirt	*1 and 2*	*Victorian*
2	a fleece with a hood	....	....
3	unisex clothes	....	....
4	a striped jacket	....	....
5	blue jeans	....	....
6	colourful clothes	....	....
7	long necklaces	....	....
8	uniforms	....	....
9	a mini-skirt	....	....
10	a baseball cap	....	....

...... *Extension activities* ....

a   To talk about
     Is it important to you to have fashionable, designer-label clothes?

b   Write 'Fashion fads' in your own words.

5 (16) Listen to the interview with a super model.

a   Answer the questions:
    1 What does Stephanie like about her job?
    2 What clothes does she usually wear?
    3 Why does she become angry?

b   Work in pairs and prepare an interview with a modern fashion designer. Student A is the interviewer and Student B is the fashion designer. Ask questions like …
    'What do you think the next fashions will be like?
    'Which are your favourite clothes today?

Extra activity
– Fancy Dress

Work in pairs. Design and draw a costume for a fancy dress party or carnival. Describe the colours and materials of your design to your partner.

9 High noon

1 'High Noon' is a favourite TV Western with Killer Clint.
Look at the pictures and tell the story.

.. *Here are some words to help you* ....

gunfighter (2)   to be frightened (3)   Sheriff (4)   saloon (5)   to hide (7)

2 **Put these sentences in order to retell the story.**

a He's drinking whisky at the bar.

b It's 12 o'clock – high noon. Killer Clint is at the Sheriff's office.
   The sherrif is hiding.

c Killer Clint is a dangerous gunfighter. He has just arrived in Desertville.

d The people of desertville are frightened. They're running away.

e What do you think will happen next?

f High Noon is a very popular TV programme about outlaws in the Wild West. `1`

g Now Killer Clint is kicking open the door of the saloon bar.

h Even the Sheriff and his Deputy are afraid of Killer Clint.

3 (17) **Listen to the story and check your answers to Exercise 2.**

4 **Answer the following questions:**

1 What does Clint look like?

2 What did the people do when Clint arrived?

3 Where did Clint go first?

4 What time did Clint go to the Sheriff's office?

5 What did the Sheriff do when he saw Clint?

6 What do you think will happen in next week's
   exciting episode?

5 (18) **Listen to the interview with the Sheriff.**

a Answer the questions:
   1 Why did Killer Clint go to Desertville?
   2 What happened to Hank?

b Work in pairs and prepare an interview with Killer Clint.
   Student A is the interviewer and Student B is Clint.
   Ask questions like …

   '*Why is everyone afraid of you?*'
   '*Do you think Hank is an innocent man?*'

Extension activities ....

a To talk about
   Do you like cowboy or Western films?
   Talk about one that you have seen.
b Write 'High noon' in your own words.

Extra activity
– Wanted!

Make a wanted poster for Killer Clint or
another Wild West outlaw. Draw a
picture of the outlaw, write a description
of him/her. Don't forget to include
a reward for his/her capture!

10 Fitness for ever!

1 Tony is overweight, but will jogging help him to get fit?
Look at the pictures and tell the story.

...*Here are some words to help you* ....

overweight (1)   to laugh (8)   to trip over (5)   to bite (6)   back ache (8)

2 Make a sentence about each picture. Use these words to help you.

1 Tony looked at himself in the .... He was very ....

2 He had a look at his 'Keep Fit' book and decided to take some .... and go jogging.

3 He started to run along the road, but some boys .... at him.

4 Two ladies were .... on the pavement.

5 Tony .... over the dog's lead.

6 Then the dog .... Tony.

7 While he was limping home it started to .... and he got very wet.

8 He was cold and miserable and he had .... He .... his 'Keep Fit' book in the bin!

> mirror
> laughed
> threw
> overweight
> tripped
> back ache
> rain
> exercise
> bit
> talking

3 (19) Listen to the story and check your answers to Exercise 2.

4 Match these words to their definitions.

1	overweight	**a**	the path beside the road
2	miserable	**b**	fat
3	trip	**c**	walk with difficulty
4	pavement	**d**	unhappy
5	limp	**e**	fall over something

MARATHON!

5 (20) Listen to the interview with a fitness fanatic.

a Answer the questions:
  1 What exercise does Bella do each day?
  2 When did she start to do so much exercise – and why?

Extension activities ....

a To talk about
   Do you think that, in general, people are fitter these days than 50 years ago?
   How do you keep fit?
b Write 'Fitness for ever!' in your own words.

Extra activity
– Sports

Take turns to mime a sport. Point to another student who must say the name of the sport. Write the sport on the board. How many sports can you collect in ten minutes?

11 Bank robbers on camera

1 These robbers attacked a bank. Will they get away with the money?
Look at the pictures and tell the story.

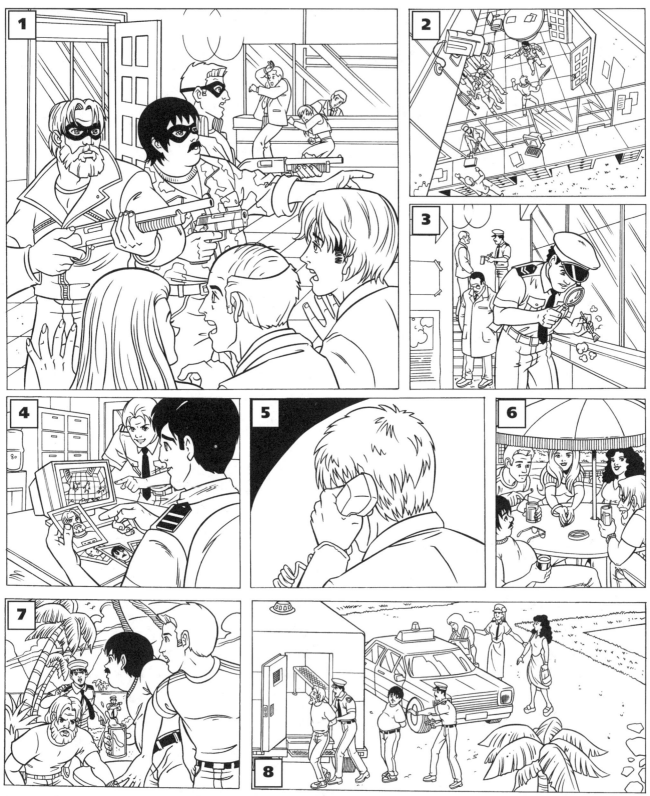

...Here are some words to help you ....

masked men (1)   security camera (2)   fingerprints (3)   an informer (5)   to arrest (6)

2 Make a sentence about each picture and retell the story. Use these words to help you.

1 Last month the three masked men terrified .... and staff at the bank.

2 However, the raid was filmed by a security ....

3 Police took statements from .... and found fingerprints.

4 The police were able to identify the .... from the film.

5 An .... telephoned the police.

6 The robbers were in the Bahamas with their ....

7 The police found them and .... them.

8 They took the robbers to the police station at ....

> robbers
> customers
> informer
> camera
> gunpoint
> girlfriends
> arrested
> witnesses

3 (21) Listen to the story and check your answers to Exercise 2

4 Fill in the blanks to complete these definitions.

villa   cashier   witnesses   criminals   bulletin   statement

1 A news report is sometimes called a ....

2 A type of house often used for holidays is a ....

3 Somebody who works in a bank behind the counter is a ....

4 People who see a crime and give information to the police are ....

5 The information that witnesses give to the police is called a ....

6 Robbers are types of ....

5 (22) Listen to the interview with one of the robber's girlfriends.
a Answer the questions:
   1 Where did Nigella meet Shotgun Sid?
   2 What did he tell her about his job?
   3 Did she see his picture in the paper?

b Work in pairs and prepare an interview with a police officer. Student A is the interviewer and Student B is the police officer. Ask questions like …

'Who did you talk to?'
'How did you find the robbers?'

Extra Activity
– Statements

In pairs, imagine you were witnesses at the bank robbery. Write a statement for the police. When did you arrive at the bank? What did you see? What did you do?

Extension activities

a To talk about
   You are the Judge. How long should these bank robbers spend in prison?
b Write 'Bank robbers on camera' in your own words.

12 Carry on camping

1 This family went on a camping holiday. But everything went wrong.
Look at the pictures and tell the story.

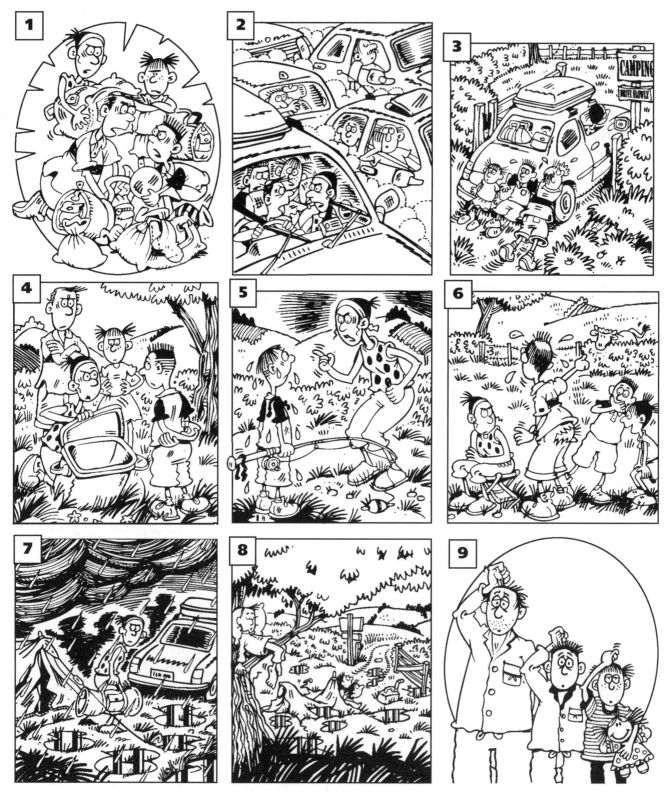

.. *Here are some words to help you* ....

to pack (1)   to run out of petrol (2)   picnic (4)   to fall in (6)   to drive off (8)

2 Join the two halves to make full sentences and retell the story.

1 The Thompsons packed

2 The traffic was very bad

3 Then they ran out

4 They decided to have a picnic but

5 Then Alex went fishing

6 Mr Thompson was chased

7 In the night there was a storm

8 The tent collapsed and

a of petrol and had to push the car to the campsite.

b by a bull and tore his trousers.

c and Mrs Thompson decided to go home.

d Mr Thompson slept in a tree.

e and they were stuck in a traffic jam.

f Alex had eaten all the food.

g everything for a camping holiday.

h and fell in the lake.

3 (23) Listen to the story and check your answers to Exercise 2.

4 Circle the correct answer.

a You have an argument when you agree / disagree with somebody.

b In a traffic jam, the cars are moving fast / standing still.

c A campsite is a place where you put up a tent / have a picnic.

d When you run out of petrol, you have no petrol / lots of petrol.

e A bull is a male cow / sheep.

f Mr Thompson tore his trousers on a fence / wall.

g At the end of the story the tent blew away / collapsed.

5 (24) Listen to the interview with Mr and Mrs Thompson.

a Answer the questions:
1 What was the worst thing for Mr Thompson?
2 What was the worst thing for Mrs Thompson?
3 Do they have any holiday plans for next year?

b Work in pairs and prepare an interview with Alex. Student A is the interviewer and Student B is Alex. Ask questions like …

'Did you enjoy the camping holiday?'
'What happened to you?'

Extra activity
– Packing

You are going on a camping holiday. In small groups write a listof things you need to take. Compare your list with another group. What are the 10 most important things to take?

....*Extension activities* ....

a To talk about
Have you ever been on a camping holiday?
What are the advantages and disadvantages of a camping holiday?

b Write 'Carry on camping' in your own words.

13 Earthquake hits city

1 Two years ago there was a terrible earthquake in Kanahz.
Look at the pictures and tell the story.

.. *Here are some words to help you* ....

to collapse (1)   to be trapped (2)   rescuers (3)   broadcast (4)   charity appeal (6)

2 Make a sentence about each picture and retell the story. Use these words to help you.

1 The earth began to .... and buildings collapsed.

2 There were fires and people were .... in the buildings.

3 .... tried to help people get out.

4 The .... broadcast said that a thousand people were dead.

5 Tents, blankets and .... came in from other countries.

6 There were charity appeals to .... money for Kanahz.

7 Some aid was stolen and sold on the ....

8 After some time help came to Kanahz and .... started.

9 Two years later there are new .... in the city but many

   people still live in .... in the mountains.

> raise
> black market
> rebuilding
> shake
> news
> trapped
> rescuers
> medicine
> buildings
> tents

3 (25) Listen to the story and check your answers to Exercise 2.

4 Match these words to their definitions.

1 collapsed   a broken buildings
2 ruins   b people caught in a disaster
3 survivors   c fell down
4 homeless   d far away
5 remote   e a terrible and sad event
6 scandal   f people who live through a disaster
7 victims   g a shocking event
8 tragedy   h without a home
9 crooks   i bad people

5 (26) Listen to the interview with a local businessman.
   a Answer the questions:
      1 How have people made money?
      2 How much aid reached the disaster area?
      3 Was the businessman involved?
   b Work in pairs and prepare an interview with a survivor. Student A
      is the interviewer and Student B is the survivor. Ask questions like …

   'Where were you on the night of the earthquake?'
   'How did you escape?'

.. *Extension activities* ....

   a To talk about
      What natural disasters have you read about in the last few years?
      Have you raised money to help disaster victims?

   b Write 'Earthquake hits city' in your own words.

Extra activity
– The radio appeal

In small groups prepare
a one-minute radio appeal
on behalf of disaster victims.
Decide your priorities –
health, food, shelter, etc.

14 Treasure restored

1 The Metropolitan Museum in New York has a priceless collection of Greek vases. At an auction recently it bought a vase with a very interesting history. Look at the pictures and tell the story.

.. *Here are some words to help you* ....

    potter (1) vineyard (3) wreck (7) restorer (9) auction (10)

2   **Make a sentence about each picture and retell the story. Use these words to help you.**

1   About the year 300 BC, an Athenian .... made a beautiful vase.

2   It was used for carrying water or wine in the house of a .... nobleman.

3   About 2000 years later it was found by workers harvesting grapes in a ....

4   Miraculously the vase was ....

5   It was sold to a .... for very little money.

6   The merchant took the vase away with him on his ....

7   Unfortunately during the sea voyage the ship was ....

8   Last year the vase was found by a team of ....

9   A .... has carefully pieced the fragments together.

10   At an .... the vase was finally purchased for £150,000.

11   It is now in a .... in New York.

> restorer
> wealthy
> vineyard
> potter
> wrecked
> auction
> undamaged
> museum
> merchant
> ship
> divers

Did you guess the missing picture?

3   (27) **Listen to the story and check your answers to Exercise 2.**

4   **Match these words to their definitions.**

1 seaweed —   **a** a journey by sea
2 vineyard   **b** a plant that grows in the sea
3 merchant   **c** bought
4 auction   **d** a person who buys and sells things
5 voyage   **e** a person who carefully rebuilds something from broken pieces
6 restorer   **f** public sale to the person offering the highest amount
7 purchased   **g** the place where grapes are grown

5   (28) **Listen to the interview with a young visitor to the gallery.**

   a   Answer the questions:
     1 Is the visitor impressed by the display?
     2 What does she want to see next?

   b   Work in pairs and prepare an interview with the merchant. Student A is the interviewer and Student B is the merchant. Ask questions like …

     'Who did you buy the vase from?'
     'How did you lose it?'

Extra activity
– The auction

In small groups, choose an object to auction. One person is the 'auctioneer'. All players have £1,000. One of the objects is a reproduction. The auctioneer decides which is the reproduction – but does not tell the bidders until after the sale!

Extension activities

   a   To talk about
     Rich and powerful countries have taken, or bought cheaply, thousands of art treasures. Should these be returned to their countries of origin?
   b   Write 'Treasure restored' in your own words.

15 A week in paradise

1 Tom and Judy have just returned from their honeymoon. They told us 'It was a holiday we will never forget.' Look at the pictures and tell the story.

.. *Here are some words to help you* ....

to get married (2)   factories (4)   polluted (6)   in plaster (9)   travel agents (11)

2 Make a sentence about each picture and retell the story. Use these words to help you.

1   They spent a lot of time looking for the .... honeymoon.

2   They had a wonderful .... day and were looking forward to going away.

3   They set off the day after their wedding but their .... was delayed.

4   When they arrived, they were .... because it was cold and rainy.

5   From their room, they had a view of ugly ....

6   The beach was dirty and the sea was ....

7   Tom .... on a wall while Judy took his photo.

8   Unfortunately, he .... off the wall.

9   He went to hospital and his leg was put in ....

10 Judy spent most of the time writing ....

11 Tom .... read magazines.

12 Back home, Tom is going to the Travel Agents to ....!

> perfect
> polluted
> disappointed
> posed
> gloomily
> wedding
> postcards
> plaster
> complain
> plane
> factories
> slipped

3 (29) Listen to the story and check your answers to Exercise 2.

4 Which words in the story mean ...?

1   a high standard of comfort   ....

2   away from the sea   ....

3   miserably   ....

4   to stand or sit for a photograph   ....

5   to be late   ....

5 (30) Listen to the interview with the Travel Agent.

a   Answer the questions:
    1 Is the Travel Agent sympathetic?
    2 Will Tom and Judy get any compensation?

b   Work in pairs and prepare an interview with Judy.
    Student A is the interviewer and Student B is Judy.

    Ask questions like …

    'Did you enjoy your honeymoon?'
    'How is Tom now?'

Did you guess the missing picture?

Extra activity
– The holiday

In small groups prepare a poster for an amazing holiday in a very unusual location. The class votes for the best holiday.

..... **Extension activities** ....

a   To talk about
    Have you ever had a disappointing holiday? What happened?
b   Write 'A week in paradise' in your own words.

16 Olympic success story

1 Lisa is a bright star in the world of athletics. What does the future hold for her?
Look at the pictures and tell the story.

.. *Here are some words to help you* ....

champion (2)   to train (3)   to injure (6)   welcome (9)   coach (6)

2 Put the sentences in order to retell the story.

a She won the Silver Medal. ☐

b She was hit by a motorcyclist. ☐

c She trained very hard. ☐

d She injured her arm. ☐

e Despite the pain she ran in the 5000 m race. ☐

f Now she is a coach at the National Stadium. ☐

g She gained a place in the team for the Olympics. ☐

h The President gave a grand reception in her honour. ☐

i At fifteen she became National Junior athletics Champion. ☐

j She received a tremendous welcome when she returned home. ☐

k Lisa used to race her friends to and from school every day. 1

l Lisa is very popular and is thinking of becoming a politician. ☐

Did you guess the missing picture?

3 (31) Listen to the story and check your answers to Exercise 2.

4 Which words in the story mean …

1 a person who teaches a sport? ....

2 the winner? ....

3 to hurt? ....

4 shouting and calling out? ....

5 a big party ....

5 (32) Listen to the interview with the motorcyclist.

a Answer the questions:
  1 Whose fault was the accident?
  2 Has he seen Lisa since the accident?

b Work in pairs and prepare an interview with a sports fan. Student A is the interviewer and Student B is the sports fan. Ask questions like …

  'Did you watch the race?'
  'Were you happy with the result?'

Extension activities

a To talk about
  Which olympic sports do you like?
  What do you think of the Olympic Games?
b Write 'Olympic success story' in your own words.

Extra activity
– Olympic planners

You are members of the Olympic Committee. You need to cut four events from the next Olympics. In small groups decide which of the following sports to omit: archery, boxing, cycling, equestrian (dressage), football, rowing, pistol shooting, synchronised swimming, water polo, yachting. Compare your choices with other groups.

17 Lottery win

1 After only six months of the 'high life', ex-waitress Vera Binks, winner of the £1,250,000
lottery 'jackpot', started work again today – in the kitchen of her own café.
Look at the pictures and tell the story.

.: *Here are some words to help you* ....

to win (1)   begging letters (4)   to flirt (7)   to be heartbroken (8)   to decorate (11)

2 Make a sentence about each picture. Use these words to help you.

1 Vera and Jack were childhood ....

2 Things changed .... when Vera won a million and a quarter pounds.

3 She got a lot of attention from the ....

4 She received hundreds of .... letters.

5 She started going to cocktail parties and fell for a .... and wealthy man.

6 He .... with her and flattered her.

7 She spent a fortune on designer clothes and beauty ....

8 When her new lover left her she was ....

9 She started to drink .... and take anti-depressants.

10 She went back to see Jack. He was .... to make a fresh start.

11 Vera bought the café and had it ....

12 Vera and Jack are happy to be working .... again.

> alcohol
> flirted
> delighted
> overnight
> treatments
> handsome
> press
> begging
> decorated
> heartbroken
> sweethearts
> together

Did you guess the missing picture?

3 (33) Listen to the story and check your answers to Exercise 2.

4 What words in the story mean ...

1 desperately asking for money? ....

2 to say nice things to someone to get something from them? ....

3 aim in life? ....

4 young lovers? ....

5 a lot of money? ....

5 (34) Listen to the interview with Jack.

a Answer the questions:
1 Did Jack stay in touch with Vera after she won the money?
2 Has she fully recovered yet?

b Work in pairs and prepare an interview with Vera. Student A is the interviewer and Student B is Vera. Ask questions like ...

'What was it like to win so much money?'
'How do you feel now?'

Extra activity
– The begging letter
Work in small groups. Each group represents different organisations. Plan and write a letter to Vera Binks asking for financial support for a specific project. Explain why your project needs money. The class then represents Vera and decides which projects to support.

Extension activities ....

a To talk about
Is the lottery a good thing or a bad thing? What would you do if you won £500,000 tomorrow?
b Write 'Lottery win' in your own words.

18 Solo career

1 Mike Nasal, former lead guitarist with Volcano, has just made No. 1 in the charts with his new solo disc. Look at the pictures and tell the story.

.:. *Here are some words to help you* ....

smash hit (2)   to be mobbed (5)   to be stressed out (6)   to split up (9)   to drown (10)

2 Correct the sentences about each picture to retell the story. Use these words to help.

1 Volcano is the name of a popular mountain.

2 Their smash hit, 'Fire for you', made them angry.

3 Their energetic stage show was a sell out on their world holiday.

4 During their tour, they danced in cities from New York to Sydney.

5 After each concert, they were mobbed by whispering fans.

6 They were lively and stressed out by the end of the tour.

7 Jake started taking photos.

8 Belle and Mike had a violent hug.

9 Soon afterwards, the group disappeared.

10 Jake was found drowned in the toilet of his mansion after a party.

11 Dessi and Belle went in search of noise and are now living in a remote cottage.

12 Mike now has a useless career as a solo artist.

exhausted
split up
tour
pop group
screaming
famous
drugs
performed
argument
swimming pool
peace
successful

3 (35) Listen to the story and check your answers to Exercise 2.

4 What words in the story mean ...?

1 to be attacked (often by people who like you) ....

2 to finish a relationship ....

3 to love/admire excessively ....

4 a very sad event ....

5 extremely tired ....

6 when all tickets for a show are sold ....

Did you guess the missing picture?

5 (36) Listen to the interview with Mike.

a Answer the questions:
1 How does Mike feel about Volcano?
2 Does he keep in touch with the other members of the band?

b Work in pairs and prepare an interview with Dessi.
Student A is the interviewer and Student B is Dessi.
Ask questions like ...

'Where are you living now?'
'Do you miss your time with Volcano?'

Extra activity
– Top ten hits

Work in small groups.
Each group is a recording company,
which is going to release a CD of
all-time greatest hits. Choose
ten songs with the names of
the recording artists. Tell your
'Top ten' choice to the other
groups. Is it possible to agree
a best selection?

.. Extension activities ....

a To talk about
Do you know any pop groups that have split up?
Do you think some stars have problems because they are too young?
b Write 'Solo career' in your own words.

19 Endangered species

1 In many countries animals are in danger from hunters and poachers. What should be done to save them? Look at the pictures and tell the story.

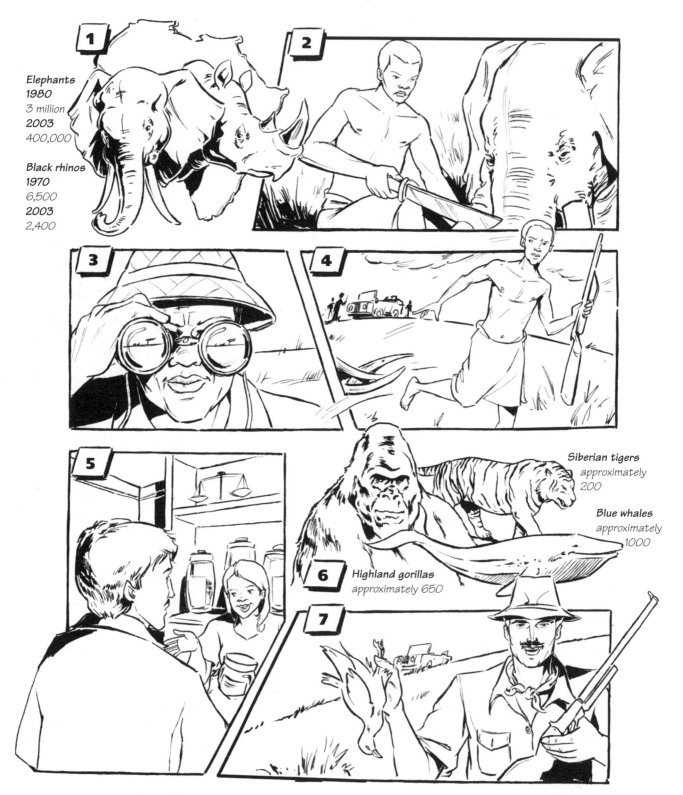

1

Elephants
1980
3 million
2003
400,000

Black rhinos
1970
6,500
2003
2,400

Siberian tigers
approximately
200

Blue whales
approximately
1000

Highland gorillas
approximately 650

.. *Here are some words to help you* ....

endangered animals (1)   tusks (2)   game wardens (3)   traditional medicine (5)   hunters (7)

2   **Join the two halves to make full sentences and retell the story.**

1 Elephants and rhinos are two of   **a** are killed every year for 'sport'.

2 They are killed   **b** the most endangered animals in Africa.

3 Game Wardens try to   **c** before they harm the animals.

4 They try to catch the poachers   **d** protect the animals.

5 Rhino's horns are regarded as having   **e** special powers in Chinese medicine.

6 Other endangered species are   **f** gorillas, tiger and whales.

7 In some European countries, small birds   **g** for their tusks or horns.

3   (37) **Listen to the story and check your answers to Exercise 2.**

4   **What words in the story mean ...?**

1 to kill   ....

2 against the law   ....

3 to go bad   ....

4 the material tusks are made of   ....

5 a group of elephants/rhinos, etc. ....

6 powerful guns   ....

5   (38) **Listen to the interview with a conservationist.**

a Answer the questions:
   1 Which animals do they look after?
   2 What eventually happens to them?
   3 Are rhinos more or less difficult to send back to the wild?

b Work in pairs and prepare an interview with a holidaymaker going on Safari in Africa. Student A is the interviewer and Student B is the holidaymaker.
Ask questions like ...

'Which animals do you hope to see today?'
'How will you travel through the game park?'

Extra activity
– Animals in danger

In groups, choose an endangered species. Find out more about the species. As a class, stick pictures and statistics about your species on a world map indicating where the animals come from.

.... *Extension activities* ....

a To talk about
Is hunting popular in your country? Which animals can be killed?
What do you think about hunting?
b Write 'Endangered species' in your own words.

20 The end of smallpox

1 This is a success story for medicine – but lots more problems remain. Look at the pictures and tell the story.

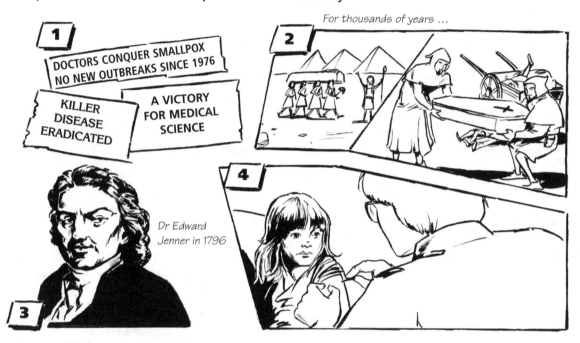

For thousands of years …

1

DOCTORS CONQUER SMALLPOX
NO NEW OUTBREAKS SINCE 1976

KILLER
DISEASE
ERADICATED

A VICTORY
FOR MEDICAL
SCIENCE

2

3

Dr Edward Jenner in 1796

4

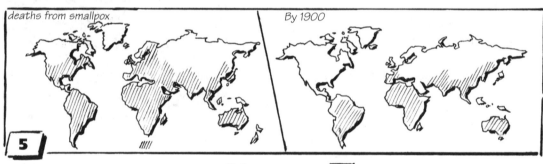

Before vaccination

deaths from smallpox

By 1900

5

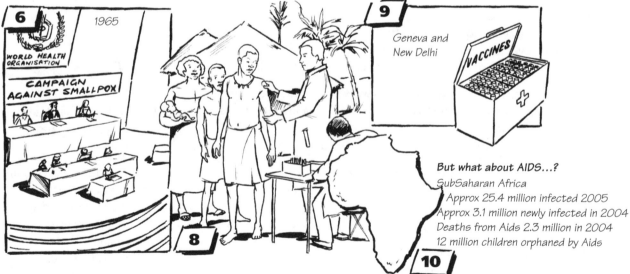

6   1965

WORLD HEALTH
ORGANISATION

CAMPAIGN
AGAINST SMALLPOX

8

9

*Geneva and
New Delhi*

VACCINES

But what about AIDS…?
SubSaharan Africa
Approx 25.4 million infected 2005
Approx 3.1 million newly infected in 2004
Deaths from Aids 2.3 million in 2004
12 million children orphaned by Aids

10

.. *Here are some words to help you* ....

discover (1)   to vaccinate (4)   outbreaks of disease (5)   vaccination campaign (6)   stores (8)

2 Make a sentence about each picture and retell the story. Use these words to help you.

1   Medical science has .... smallpox.

2   This terrible disease has been ....

3   A British doctor, Edward Jenner discovered the smallpox .... in 1796.

4   He .... people with a vaccine and their bodies to built up resistance.

5   By 1900 there was almost no smallpox in Europe and North America, but

.... of the disease continued in South America, Asia and Africa.

6   In 1965, the World Health Organisation began a vaccination .... to eradicate smallpox.

7   Teams of doctors have vaccinated millions of people even in .... areas.

8   Huge stores of vaccine are kept in Geneva and New Delhi in case of ....

9   But we are still at .... from killer diseases such as SARS and AIDS.

> outbreaks
> conquered
> injected
> emergency
> eradicated
> vaccine
> campaign
> remote
> risk

3   **39** Listen to the story and check your answers to Exercise 2.

4   Circle the correct answer.

1   Smallpox is a (country, disease, science).

2   A sudden appearance or beginning of something bad is called a(n) (headline, outbreak, vaccine).

3   A discoverer (finds, kills, opens) something.

4   If you build up resistance to a disease you (can, can't, have to) get sick from it.

5   A team is a group of people who (work, eat, live) together.

5   **40** Listen to the interview with a doctor in Africa.

a Answer the questions:
   1 What does he like about the work?
   2 What doesn't he like?

b Work in pairs and prepare an interview with a villager. Student A
   is the interviewer and Student B is the villager.
   Ask questions like …

   'How does the doctor help people in your village?'
   'What other things does your village need to make life easier?'

Extra activity
– Health laws

Work in small groups. You are the Government Minister for Health. You can introduce five laws to raise the general level of physical and mental health in your country. What will you introduce? Compare your list with the 'laws' from other groups.

.... *Extension activities* ....

a To talk about
   You are the Government. A company has discovered a vaccine which can extend life by an average of ten years. Will you allow this vaccine to be sold?
b Write 'The end of smallpox' in your own words.

21 Taking water to the desert

1 Prince Faisal's imaginative idea, an investment of millions of pounds, is bringing new life to the desert. Look at the pictures and tell the story.

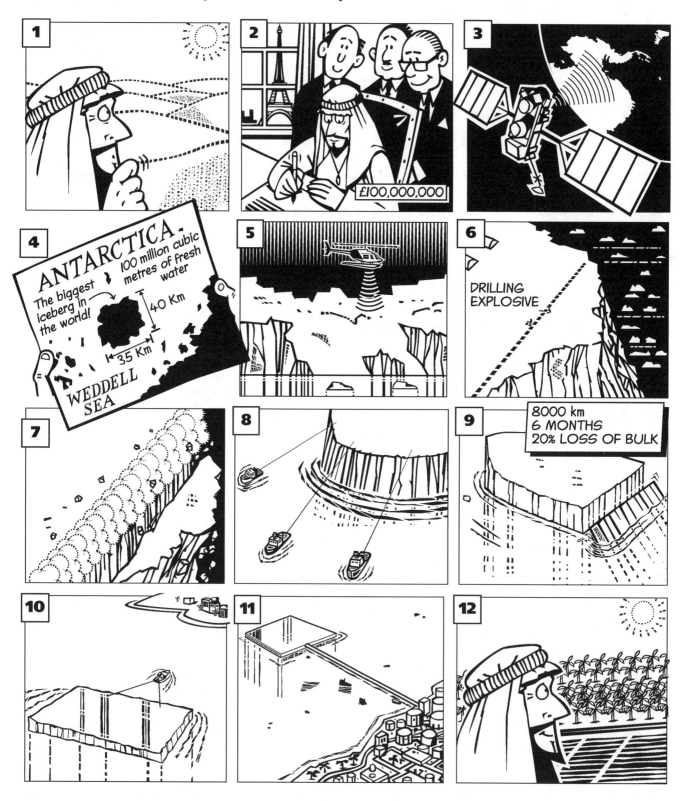

.. *Here are some words to help you* ....

desert (1)   consortium (2)   to tow (8)   blocks (10)   to pump ashore (11)   to irrigate (12)

2 Make a sentence about each picture and retell the story. Use these words to help you.

1 Prince Faisal had an .... idea.

2 He signed a £100,000,000 contract with a .... of investors in Paris.

3 A .... was used to survey Antarctica.

4 They decided that the biggest iceberg in the world would be ....

5 The iceberg was tested to make sure it would not ....

6 Holes were drilled into the .... of the iceberg.

7 Explosives were used to .... the iceberg into shape.

8 A fleet of powerful .... began to tow it on the 8,000 kilometre journey.

9 The iceberg lost twenty per cent of its ....

10 On arrival at its .... , it was sliced into huge blocks.

11 The blocks were then towed much nearer the shore and the process of .... the ice, and pumping the water ashore through a pipeline could begin.

12 The fresh water was used to .... fields. Prince Faisal is delighted with the results.

> irrigate
> bulk
> consortium
> blast
> destination
> melting
> imaginative
> tugs
> crack
> satellite
> surface
> suitable

3 (41) Listen to the story and check your answers to Exercise 2.

4 What words in the story mean ...?

1 to provide fields with water ....

2 very, very big ....

3 a group of companies ....

4 a ship for pulling ....

5 to break with great force ....

6 to change from solid to liquid ....

Extension activities

a To talk about
Are there easier and cheaper ways of providing fresh water?
What are the problems with the iceberg idea?

b Write 'Taking water to the desert' in your own words.

5 (42) Listen to the interview with a geologist.

a Answer the questions:
1 Is the geologist in favour of or against Prince Faisal's plan?
2 What alternatives are there?

b Work in pairs and prepare an interview with a desert farmer. Student A is the interviewer and Student B is the desert farmer. Ask questions like ...

'How will you use the water from the iceberg?'
'How will the desert change?'

Extra activity
– Energy conservation

With a partner design and draw a house which shows at least seven energy saving features.

22 Microchip revolution

1 Computers have changed our lives so much. Here are some examples.
Look at the pictures and tell the story.

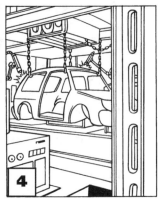

.. Here are some words to help you ....

miniature (1)   everyday items (2)   equipment (3)   robotics (4)   benefits (6)

2 Join the two halves to make full sentences and retell the story.

1 In one generation, the miniature microchip

a everyday items.

2 Computers have become compact,

b entirely beneficial?

3 Microchips are an integral part of many

c has changed life for all of us.

4 Industry relies heavily on

d and in the home for many purposes.

5 Computers are used in schools

e robotics for assembly work.

6 Has this revolution been

f affordable and very powerful.

3 (43) Listen to the story and check your answers to Exercise 2.

4 Add these sentences to the story in the correct positions.

a The motor industry is one example.

b Computers have replaced work previously done by people and they have not put an end to poverty and disease.

c In the 1960s, computers were large and expensive.

d A light-weight laptop today does a larger job than a massive computer of the 60s.

e They are also used in scanners in hospitals and in navigation instruments.

f Many people have e-mail at home and use the internet for getting information and doing the shopping.

5 (44) Listen to the interview with a commuter.

a Answer the questions:
  1 What does Mr Ludd dislike most?
  2 Is he against all electronic devices?
  3 Should Mr Ludd find another way to travel?

b Work in pairs and prepare an interview with a laptop user. Student A is the interviewer and Student B is the laptop user. Ask questions like …

'Where did you buy your computer and all the software?'
'What do you use your machine for mostly – music, films or schoolwork?'

.. *Extension activities* ....

a To talk about
In which ways has the microchip revolution affected your life – for the better? – for the worse?

b Write 'Microchip revolution' in your own words.

Extra activity
– Technological advances

In small groups, think of the ways in which computers will continue to change our lives in the following areas:
1 medicine, **2** personal transport, **3** education, **4** the home, **5** personal communication.
Compare ideas with other groups.

23 Iceland and Cuba

1 Today our Foreign Correspondent is comparing two very different islands. Look at the pictures and tell the story.

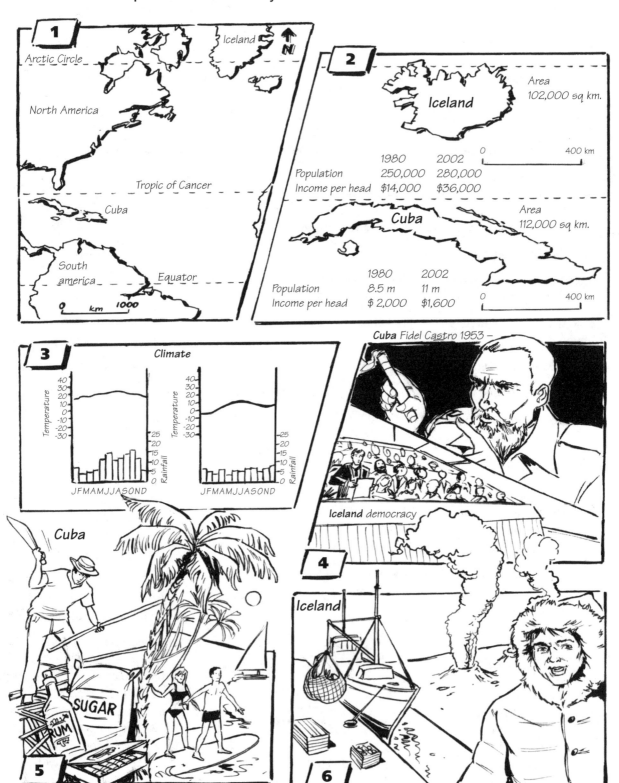

1

Iceland
Arctic Circle
North America
Tropic of Cancer
Cuba
South america
Equator
km 1000

2

Iceland   Area 102,000 sq km.

	1980	2002
Population	250,000	280,000
Income per head	$14,000	$36,000

0   400 km

Cuba   Area 112,000 sq km.

	1980	2002
Population	8.5 m	11 m
Income per head	$ 2,000	$1,600

0   400 km

3 Climate

JFMAMJJASOND   JFMAMJJASOND

Cuba

Cuba Fidel Castro 1953 –

Iceland democracy

4

Iceland

5 SUGAR   RUM

6

.:. *Here are some words to help you* ....

situated (1)   size (2)   politics (4)   natural resources (5)   tourism (6)

2 Make a sentence about each picture and retell the story. Use these words to help you.

1 Iceland is .... very far north.

2 The islands are roughly the same .... in square kilometres.

3 As you would expect from their location, the .... in the two countries is quite different.

4 The .... of the two countries are also different, with Castro in control of Cuba while Iceland is a Democratic Republic.

5 Both countries have good natural ....

6 .... and fishing are important industries in Iceland.

> politics
> size
> resources
> situated
> tourism
> climate

3 (45) Listen to the story and check your answers to Exercise 2.

4 Are these sentences true (*T*) or false (*F*)?

1 Cuba is on the Tropic of Cancer.

2 Iceland is narrower and longer than Cuba.

3 Iceland is more densely populated than Cuba.

4 Iceland has a higher income per head.

5 It is rainy in Cuba from May to November.

6 Temperatures in Iceland are never below zero.

7 Iceland is a Marxist State.

8 Sugar cane and rice are major crops in Cuba.

9 Cuban beer and Havana cigars are world famous.

10 In Iceland visitors come to see the geysers.

.. *Extension activities* ....

a To talk about
Which countries have you visited or read about? How do they compare with your country?
b Write 'Iceland and Cuba' in your own words.

5 (46) Listen to the interview with an Ambassador from an EU country.

a Answer the questions:
1 Which country is she talking about?
2 How does the economy compare with other EU countries?
3 What are the main attractions?

b Work in pairs and prepare an interview with a tourist. Student A is the interviewer and Student B is the tourist. Ask questions like …

'Where would you like to go – Iceland or Cuba?'
'What would you like to do there?'

Extra activity
– My country
Find out more about your own country. Think about these things:
1 size, **2** population,
3 average income, **4** climate,
5 politics, **6** natural resources,
7 main industries.
Draw a map and write the information on and around the map.

24 Escape from war-torn country

1 Many people are forced to leave their homes. This is the story of one of them.
Look at the pictures and tell the story.

.. *Here are some words to help you* ....

to graduate (1)   to force (2)   cargo ship (5)   stateless (6)   low-paid (11)   to settle

2 Make a sentence about each picture and retell the story. Use these words to help you.

1 Today Michael .... from college.

2 Ten years ago, Michael's family was forced out of their war-torn ....

3 They walked three hundred kilometres to .... the fighting.

4 They tried to reach .... by crossing the sea in a small boat.

5 They were rescued by a passing ....

6 They were treated as stateless people as they had no .... documents.

7 At last, they were given a .... for Canada.

8 They flew to Vancouver in ....

9 It was a .... cold day.

10 They spent the next months in a tiny room while Michael got a work ....

11 He worked hard at ...., part-time jobs and eventually was able to enrol

for a college course.

12 Now, Michael and his family are happily ....

into a new life.

> January
> visa
> settled
> identity
> escape
> low-paid
> permit
> cargo boat
> village
> bitterly
> graduated
> safety

3 (47) Listen to the story and check your answers to Exercise 2.

4 Match these words to their definitions.

1 migrants — a an invented story

2 traumatic → b people who move to another country

3 to die of exposure c without nationality

4 stateless d to die as a result of extreme weather

5 fiction e dramatic and upsetting

5 (48) Listen to the interview with a Vietnamese immigrant.

a Answer the questions:
1 When did he come to Britain?
2 What does he do for a living?
3 What are his feelings about Vietnam?

b Work in pairs and prepare an interview with Michael's child.
Student A is the interviewer and Student B is the child.
Ask questions like …

'Did your parents have a difficult time?
'Do you think of yourself as Canadian?'

Extension activities

a To talk about
Are there good reasons for
countries to accept refugees?
Are there good reasons to
refuse refugees?
b Write 'Escape from war-torn
country' in your own words.

Extra activity
– Useful phrases

Work in small groups. You are
members of a committee helping
refugees with language.
1 Make a list of the thirty
most useful phrases or sentences
in English.
2 Compare your list of useful
phrases with the other groups.
Are the lists
the same?

TAPESCRIPTS

1 Another day, another dollar

Story

James Cash is a very rich man – in fact, he's a multi-millionaire. He is thirty-five years old and lives in a mansion in the country. He is the chairman of a big company. Every day he has breakfast in bed. He usually has boiled eggs and champagne! He makes phone calls and reads the newspapers at breakfast time. Then he gets dressed. His servants help him. He always wears a smart suit to the office.

At seven o'clock his chauffeur drives him to his office. He has business meetings every morning. Every afternoon he looks at the sales reports. Sales go up every year because business is good. In the evenings he likes to entertain important business clients. They often go to his favourite night club, Madame JoJo's. They have dinner, drink champagne and watch a cabaret. At two o'clock in the morning his chauffeur drives him home. He goes to bed half an hour later, and dreams about sales figures. James is always exhausted. The next day is exactly the same. Would you want a job like his?

Interview

Interviewer:	It's well-known that Mr Cash is one of the richest men in Britain. Does he work every day?
PA:	Umm, well, he doesn't usually work on Sundays – except when he has business visitors, or a special meeting, or if he's on a business trip, or if the company is very busy … which, actually, is quite often so…
Interviewer:	So in fact he works seven days most weeks?
PA:	Yes, I suppose so – but he has a holiday every year. He goes to his villa in the south of France.
Interviewer:	And how long is his holiday?
PA:	Well, he goes for a month in August, but he usually comes back early. He says he gets bored.
Interviewer:	Why do you think he works so hard?
PA:	He loves it! The company is his life! He doesn't have anything else. It's not for me, though. I'm leaving my job next month and going travelling! There's more to life than money!

2 Environmental disaster

Story

Last night there was an accident in the South China sea, near the Philippines. An oil tanker hit a fishing boat. The collision happened in very stormy weather at half past two in the morning. The fishing boat sank, but the crew got into a life raft. The tanker didn't see the men in the life raft and didn't stop. There was a big hole in the bow of the oil tanker and thousands of tons of oil came out, and leaked into the sea. The fishermen sent up rockets and flares. A rescue boat saw them and rescued the fishermen. They gave them blankets and hot drinks but they were still very cold and shocked.

This morning, in daylight, a search helicopter saw all the oil on the sea. Special boats are spraying chemicals on the oil but the beaches are already polluted. A lot of fish and seabirds are caught in the oil. It is a very bad day indeed for the fishing and tourism industries.

Interview

Interviewer:	Pito, what was the first you knew of the danger?
Fisherman:	I was downstairs in the cabin. I was cooking some fish for me, and the others. Then, I heard a terrible smashing noise. I didn't know what it was. Then the tanker was on top of us like a big grey mountain. The next thing I knew we were all fighting for life in the cold water.
Interviewer:	Was it very difficult to get into the life raft?
Fisherman:	It was almost impossible. It was dark, the boat was sinking, and the sea was very rough. But we did it.
Interviewer:	Were you surprised that the tanker didn't stop?
Fisherman:	We sent up flares, when we were in the life raft. I'm sure they saw them, but they didn't come back for us. They don't care about a few fishermen!
Interviewer:	How are the rest of the crew feeling at the moment?
Fisherman:	Well, we're all alive, and that's something! But the worst thing is that we've lost our boat. How can we catch fish without a boat? How will we live? It's absolutely terrible.

3 Gap year

Story

Last June, after his school exams had finished, Francis bought a "World Traveller" ticket and travelled around the world. First, he flew from London to Australia. His first job was picking grapes. He also swam with sharks – something he'll never forget!

His first stop in Europe was Greece, where he visited lots of old temples. Next he travelled to Italy, where he grew a beard and ate lots of pasta! While he was waiting for a train at Pisa station, a thief stole all his money. He had to sleep outside under the stars that night.

He spent three weeks in India and took lots of photos. He travelled on to Tibet where he climbed some very high mountains, including Mount Everest. It was very cold and snowy. A few months later, he went from Hong Kong to China by boat and was seasick. In China, he hired a bike and cycled to the Great Wall. And in Brazil? He went to Rio de Janeiro for carnival week, of course. He danced all night and fell in love – for a week. This morning, ten months' later, he arrived home. His parents were very pleased to see him.

Interview

Interviewer:	Tell us about what happened last June.
Lifeguard:	Well, it's not the first time it's happened. Travellers – they think they can do what they want! They don't think about anyone else.
	That afternoon, there were very big waves but the silly idiot was swimming.
Interviewer:	Maybe, he didn't know it was dangerous?
Lifeguard:	There were "Danger" signs everywhere! My colleague was watching him through binoculars, and then he saw a shark very near the swimmer.
Interviewer:	What do you do in that situation?
Lifeguard:	You set off an alarm and then you try to get to the swimmer as quickly as possible. Two of us had to pull the boy out of the sea.
Interviewer:	Is it really dangerous?
Lifeguard:	Dangerous? Of course it's dangerous! Sharks kill several people every year.
Interviewer:	And what do you say to the people you rescue?
Lifeguard:	Well we're not polite! People who go swimming where there are Danger signs are idiots! They should be more responsible. They're not children, and we're not their parents!

4 UFO story

Story

Joe Green is a postman. He lives a very ordinary life. He works all day and meets his friends in the pub in the evening. But one summer's evening last year, something very strange happened. He was on his way home when he saw an unidentified flying object, or UFO, in the sky. Joe got out of his van, and watched it. It landed in a field near his home. The UFO was glowing, and the whole field was lit up. Joe was very curious. Were there aliens inside? He walked towards the UFO and climbed in. Then, it took off! Joe didn't know what to do. He couldn't see any aliens. He looked at the control panels in the flight deck and pushed some buttons. The UFO flew into outer space and orbited the Earth. Then it landed right back in the same field.

Joe went home and told his wife the amazing story. She didn't believe him. He decided to go to the police station and told the policeman on duty there. He didn't believe him either. Finally, Joe went to the pub and told his friends. They laughed at him. Aliens?! A UFO?! A trip into outer space?!

Joe didn't care. He knew what happened. Now he goes to the same field every night and waits for the UFO to reappear. Suddenly, his life doesn't seem quite so ordinary.

Interview

Interviewer:　Some people say that your husband is a little bit crazy. Do you agree?

Joe's wife:　Absolutely! He was such an ordinary, sensible man, before all of this UFO nonsense. Now, I never see him in the evenings! He goes out every night and spends hours looking up at the sky! He says he's waiting… waiting for the UFO to come back.

Interviewer:　Do you think the UFO will come back?

Joe's wife:　What UFO?! It's rubbish! They don't exist. You know what I think happened on that night? I think he fell asleep in the van on the way home. He dreamt the whole thing! Just a stupid dream! Husbands!

5 Football crazy

Story

It was Saturday and Saturday meant football! Jim and his dad decided to go to a match. It was between Liverpool and Munich. "Can't you do something different for once?" Jim's mum asked. She hated football.

They got to the stadium at ten to three and found their seats. The players came onto the pitch and the game started at three. It was very exciting. After twenty five minutes, Liverpool scored a goal and the crowd cheered. In the second half there was a foul by a Liverpool defender and the referee gave a penalty to Munich. The Liverpool goalkeeper saved the penalty. The Munich players and supporters were very disappointed. Liverpool won the game one-nil.

Jim and his dad were really happy. Their team had won! They got home at half past six. Jim's mum was in the kitchen. "We won, mum! It was amazing!" Jim said, "What's for dinner?" "Tomato soup. You know I don't like cooking on a Saturday!" Jim and his dad didn't care. They put their supper on a tray and went into the sitting room. The day wasn't over. They put on the TV and watched the match highlights. Jim's mum was really annoyed!

Interview

Interviewer:	Can I ask you about the game?
Fan:	It was terrible! I spent a lot of money on the airfare and the ticket and for a hotel – and the game was a disaster!
Interviewer:	Why do you think Munich lost?
Fan:	The referee was blind! He made a lot of bad decisions.
Interviewer:	But Liverpool played well, didn't they? And, Munich missed a penalty.
Fan:	Liverpool played QUITE well… but Munich were better. The missed penalty was a terrible mistake by our striker.
Interviewer:	What are you going to do now?
Fan:	Well, we're in Liverpool so we're going to have a few beers and then we're going to some clubs. It's great for music here! And tomorrow morning, we're getting the plane home.
Interviewer:	Well, have a good evening, and enjoy the rest of your time in Liverpool.

6 Mother Teresa

Story

Mother Teresa was born in 1910 in Macedonia and grew up in a small town called Skopje. She became a nun. She wanted to work with very poor people in India. She arrived in India in 1929. She went to live in Calcutta and started an organisation of nuns called the Sisters of Charity to help the poor and homeless and the dying.

The Sisters run clinics and provide shelters on the pavements of the city. Every day the Sisters walk through the crowded streets and bring back people who are ill or nearly dead. They also help children, especially orphans.

In 1979 Mother Teresa got the Nobel Prize for Peace. She accepted it in the name of the sick and homeless people of the world. She died in 1997 but her name lives on. Today, the Sisters of Charity continue to help poor people all over the world.

Interview

Interviewer: Firstly, can you tell me about your organisation?

Charity Worker: Yes we're a fairly small charity, and we help people in developing countries, especially Africa and India. Our most important job is sending planes with doctors to remote areas.

Interviewer: Planes…?

Charity Worker: Yes, you see, in some places, there are no roads. If people are sick, they often die because they can't get medical help.

Interviewer: And what's your job in the organisation?

Charity Worker: I'm in charge of fund raising. I have to get money for the charity; and of course we need a lot of money because planes, and medical supplies, are very expensive.

Interviewer: How do you get the money?

Charity Worker: We organise dinners and parties, and we raise money from the tickets. A lot of our money comes from private donations. We put adverts in the papers so people know who we are and what we do.

Interviewer: Are you paid for your work?

Charity Worker: Yes. I'm a full-time paid employee, but there are lots of people in my team who are volunteers. They give their time free because they know how important this work is. We save lives every day.

7 Dinner disaster

Story

Mr and Mrs Smith both loved cooking. Mr Smith also wanted a better job in his company. They decided it was time for a dinner party. Mr Smith phoned his new boss Mr Plummer and invited him and his wife to dinner on Friday night. On Friday afternoon, Mr and Mrs Smith spent a long time cooking a delicious dinner. They prepared fresh salmon, filled with prawns and chilli.

They laid the table with silver candles and bottles of wine. Then, they got ready. Mrs Smith put on a black evening dress and Mr Smith wore his best suit. Everything was perfect.

The Plummers arrived on time at eight o'clock. "Let's have a drink!" said Mr Smith. They all went into the dining room. Then they saw the table and they were horrified. The main plate was empty. The salmon had gone! Mrs Smith burst into tears. "Don't worry, love! We can still have fish!" and Mr Smith rushed out of the house.

He ran to the Fish and Chip shop down the road and bought four portions of fish and chips. The great British takeaway! And they all had a lovely evening. So did their pet cat …

Interview

Interviewer:	Have you ever been to the Smiths' before?
Mrs Plummer:	No. Last Friday was the first time.
Interviewer:	Why was the evening unusual?
Mr Plummer:	Well, we arrived on time, said 'hello', and a few minutes later our hostess was in tears!
Mrs. Plummer:	I felt so sorry for them. George is Dave Smith's boss – so it was very embarrassing for them! When we went into the dining room the table looked beautiful, but there was no dinner! Just a very happy cat!
Mr Plummer:	Yes. Poor things – but Dave reacted very quickly – just ten minutes later we were all enjoying fish and chips!
Interviewer:	Do you have any cats?
Mrs Plummer:	We don't have a cat but we do have a very old dog – and a long time ago something similar happened to us. The dog ate our Sunday lunch!
Mr Plummer:	Anyway – it was a good evening – and we've invited Dave and Isobel to dinner with us in a few weeks time – and I'll make sure our dog is somewhere safely out of the way!

8 Fashion fads

Story

You can see from the pictures that fashions change a lot. In the Victorian times clothes were more formal than they are now. Men wore heavy jackets and trousers with neat creases. Ladies wore dresses with very full skirts. Their sportswear was very similar to ordinary clothes but men wore striped jackets and caps for tennis and women wore long dresses and hats. In the 1920s clothes were much looser. The 'Flappers', as they were called, wore expensive clothes and the women often wore long necklaces. During the wartime, of course, lots of people wore uniforms. By the 1960s many women wore mini-skirts. Men's clothing became more colourful and unusual. Everyone's clothes were more casual. Ten years later, clothes for men and women were similar. This style was called unisex and it was the age of blue jeans. Nowadays young people often wear either fleeces with hoods or baseball caps and you see a lot of body piercings or tattoos.

In the last hundred years 'Western' style clothes have become common all over the world.

Interview

Interviewer:	Hi Stephanie. Your picture is on the front of lots of magazines around the world. Is that what you like most about the job?
Stephanie:	Yes. I love the publicity – and the money of course! It's great to be a celebrity!
Interviewer:	But one article recently said you are too skinny – and you are setting a bad example to young girls. It says young girls are starving themselves to look like you. Some are becoming anorexic …
Stephanie:	That's nonsense. Absolute rubbish! What a stupid idea! I'm not too thin! To be a fashion model you have to be slim. You have to look good in the clothes – it's part of the job.
Interviewer:	And do you usually wear the designer clothes that you model?
Stephanie:	When I'm working I do but when I'm at home relaxing, I usually wear casual clothes like T-shirts and shorts or jeans.
Interviewer:	Now, what about your love-life? We hear you are seeing a lot of the rock star Mike Strum. Is that true? Is it serious?
Stephanie:	It's very difficult to keep my private life private. [irritated] You journalists are always trying to get hot stories, aren't you? Yes. Mike and I are seeing each other – but that's all I'm saying at the moment. Sorry – my agent is calling me. I have to go. The helicopter is on its way to take me to a fashion shoot.

9 High noon

Story

High Noon is a very popular TV programme. Lots of people watch it every week. It's about outlaws in the Wild West. Killer Clint is a dangerous gunfighter. He has a big black moustache and always carries two guns. He looks mean and aggressive. In today's programme, he has just got off the train at Desertville. Everyone is frightened; even the Sheriff and his Deputy. The people of the town are running away. Now Killer Clint is kicking open the door of the saloon bar. He's drinking whisky at the bar. Now it is twelve o'clock – High Noon. Killer Clint is on his way to the Sheriff's office. The Sheriff and his Deputy are hiding. They're terrified. Oh no! That's the end of today's programme! What do you think will happen next? Will there be a shoot out? Don't forget to watch next week's exciting episode.

Interview

Interviewer:	How did you feel when you heard Clint was in town?
Sheriff:	Well, everybody was obviously very frightened. I tried to keep everyone calm.
Interviewer:	Really? Why was he in Desertville that afternoon?
Sheriff:	Last month I arrested his cousin, Hank and put him in prison. He was in a fight in the saloon. When I saw Hank in the fight, I knew it was his fault.
Interviewer:	Why is that?
Sheriff:	That whole family is trouble.
Interviewer:	So what happened when Clint came into your office?
Sheriff:	He said, 'Let my cousin go now. I'll shoot your deputy if you don't.' I had to let Hank go but we'll arrest him again.

10 Fitness for ever!

Story

Tony looked at himself in the mirror. He was very overweight with a big stomach. He had a look at his 'Keep Fit' book and decided to take some exercise and go jogging. He put on his shorts and running vest and started to run along the road. Some boys laughed at him because he was running so slowly. Two ladies were talking on the pavement. One of them had a dog. Tony tripped over the dog's lead. While he was getting up the dog bit him. Its owner got very angry with Tony. While he was limping home it started to rain and he got very wet. He stood in his room feeling miserable. He was cold and wet and he had backache. He had a cut on his knee and a bite on his arm. He decided that exercise was too dangerous and threw his 'Keep Fit' book in the wastepaper bin!

Interview

Interviewer:	I'm in the Mega Fitness Centre to meet a very regular user, Bella Bouncy. Bella, it's eight o'clock in the morning, what time did you get here?
Bella:	I get here at six every morning – as soon as it's open. I'm always the first.
Interviewer:	You mean you get up before six every day to come to the Fitness Centre?
Bella:	Oh, yes, I get up at about five because I like to run to the Centre … that's about ten kilometres.
Interviewer:	And what do you do when you get here.
Bella:	I have a programme of exercises. I use the cycles and the rowing machines, then I do some weight training – and then I go to the pool and swim forty lengths.
Interviewer:	But why do you do so much exercise?
Bella:	Well, it gives me a good appetite for breakfast! No, seriously, I was very ill three years ago. I had to start exercising when I left hospital to build up my strength. Now it's part of my life – you could say I'm a fitness fanatic. Excuse me now; I'm going for a swim and then I'm going to cycle to work. I'll be back here again at six o'clock for my Jazz Dance class and then aerobics! Bye.
Interviewer:	Bye Bella … phew … I'm exhausted just talking to her. I'm going home to lie down!

11 Bank robbers on camera

Story

Here is a news bulletin. The bank robbers who stole five million pounds from City Bank last month are now under arrest. The three masked men terrified customers and staff at the bank when they forced cashiers to hand over money at gunpoint. Fortunately, the raid was filmed by a security camera. The police investigating the robbery took statements from witnesses. They were able to give good descriptions of the gunmen. Detectives also found fingerprints at the scene of the crime. The police were easily able to identify the criminals from the film, the descriptions given by witnesses and the fingerprints. An informer telephoned the police and told them that the robbers were in the Bahamas. The police found them with their girlfriends by the pool of a villa. They arrested them and took them to the local police station at gun point. They will be sent back to this country soon and will probably go to prison for a long time. There is no information yet about the five million pounds.

Interview

Interviewer:	Nigella, you were at the villa when the police arrested Shotgun Sid. How long have you known him?
Nigella:	Just for a couple of weeks. We met in a night club on a Greek island. He seemed a nice guy. He had lots of money. We had a good time together and he invited me for a holiday at his villa. It seemed like a good idea at the time.
Interviewer:	Did you know he was a bank robber?
Nigella:	Of course not! He told me he was a very successful dentist in London.
Interviewer:	And what about the others?
Nigella:	He said that one was a doctor, and the other was a retired Chief of Police.
Interviewer:	And did you really believe him?
Nigella:	Certainly. Why would he lie to me?
Interviewer:	But didn't you read about the robbery in the papers or see the pictures on TV?
Nigella:	I don't read newspapers very much. I'm more interested in clubbing …

12 Carry on camping

Story

The Thompsons, Lucy and Alex and their parents, packed everything for a camping holiday. This was the first time they had been camping and it was not easy to get everything in the car. There were a lot of arguments!

On the journey the traffic was very bad and they were stuck in a traffic jam. There were more family arguments. They were getting hot and bored. Then they ran out of petrol about half a kilometre from the campsite so they pushed the car the rest of the way. They decided to eat their picnic but there was no picnic. Alex ate all the food while the others unpacked the car. How greedy! Mr and Mrs Thompson and Lucy were very angry with Alex! Alex decided to go fishing and fell in the lake. His mother was very angry again. After that a bull chased Mr Thompson, and Mr Thompson tore his trousers on a fence. This was not a good start to their first camping holiday. In the night there was a storm; it rained very hard. Mrs Thompson said 'Enough is enough' and decided to go home. She quietly took her bag and drove off leaving everyone else behind. The tent collapsed in the night ... Mr Thompson slept in a tree. What will they do now?

Interview

Interviewer: I understand that you had a terrible holiday. What was the worst thing about it?

Mr Thompson: The bull was scary! The night in the tree was terrible. But the worst thing was finding that my wife, and the car, weren't there in the morning!

Mrs Thompson: Oh come on! It was your idea to go camping. I knew it would be a disaster. I wanted to go to a hotel in Spain!

Interviewer: And what was the worst thing for you?

Mrs Thompson: When I came back for them the next day everything was soaking wet and muddy. It took me three days to get everything clean again.

Interviewer: So why did you go camping?

Mr Thompson: I remember when I was a boy – we went camping every year – and it was always good fun! We were unlucky this time but I'm sure it will be better next year!

Mrs Thompson: I don't believe you just said that! I'm certainly not going to go camping again – ever! Next year it'll be a hotel in Spain, and probably I'll go on my own!

13 Earthquake hits city

Story

Two years ago a terrible earthquake hit the town of Kanahz.

At three o'clock in the morning the earth began to shake, great gaps appeared in the roads and buildings collapsed. Many people were trapped in the ruins. Fires broke out and swept through the town. Rescuers searched for survivors and pulled them to safety. A news broadcast told the world of the disaster – approximately a thousand people had died and ten thousand had been made homeless. Emergency aid, including tents, blankets and medicine, poured in from around the world but Kanahz is extremely remote and the trip from the nearest airport took two to three days. There were numerous charity appeals and events to raise money to help the victims of the disaster. Soon after, news broke of a dreadful scandal. Crooks had stolen a large amount of the aid and were selling it on the black market! After some time it was possible to airlift bulldozers to the site and begin clearing away the rubble. Rebuilding has now begun and there are some new buildings in the city. However, many of the earthquake victims are still living in tents in the nearby hills. Already the outside world has begun to forget about the Kanahz tragedy.

Interview

Interviewer: Is it true that hundreds of people have made money from selling aid to Kanahz on the black market?

Businessman: Some medicine and so on has been sold to the public unofficially. That's true.

Interviewer: It's estimated that only 25% of the aid given to the victims reached the disaster area. Isn't that a disgraceful scandal?

Businessman: I think those figures are exaggerated. Probably that aid was never sent to Kanahz in the first place.

Interviewer: Were you involved in the black market sales of relief aid for Kanahz?

Businessman: Certainly not – but in a country like this everyone has to look after their own family first. You have to make money any way you can.

14 Treasure restored

Story

About the year 300 BC, an expert Athenian potter made a beautiful vase. It was used for carrying water or wine in the house of a wealthy nobleman. Time passed, and the vase was lost. About 2,000 years later, it was discovered by workers who were harvesting grapes in a vineyard. Miraculously the vase was undamaged, and it was eagerly bought by a merchant for a very low price. The merchant took it away with him on his ship as he thought he could sell it for a lot of money. Unfortunately during the sea voyage there was a very bad storm and the ship was wrecked. The vase, together with the rest of the ship's contents, sank to the bottom of the sea. Last year it was found, badly damaged and covered in seaweed, by a team of divers exploring the wreck. An expert restorer has painstakingly pieced the fragments together and the distinctive design is almost as good as new. There was a lot of interest in the vase at an auction two months ago and many people bid for it. The vase was finally purchased for £150,000. It is now on display in the Greek Pottery Gallery of the Metropolitan Museum of New York.

Interview

Interviewer: What do you think of the Greek Pottery exhibition?

Young visitor: It's really boring. Hundreds of old pots. They're all the same.

Interviewer: Did you know that the museum has just paid £150,000 for this vase?

Young visitor: That's incredible! I bought my mother a vase for her birthday. She puts flowers in it. It cost £5!

Interviewer: But this one is more than two thousand years old.

Young visitor: That's what makes it even more ridiculous. The vase I bought was brand new – and the colours are much nicer. Excuse me. I want to get to a more interesting bit of the museum. The Egyptian mummies are much more fun!

15   A week in paradise

Story

Tom and Judy got married two weeks ago. Before they got married, they spent a long time choosing where to have a perfect honeymoon. They chose Paradise Island because they wanted a luxury hotel, the opportunity for sunbathing on superb beaches, swimming in the clear blue water and plenty of lively nightlife to enjoy.

Their wedding day was wonderful and they were looking forward to their holiday. They set off early the next day but unfortunately their plane was delayed. They weren't too worried because they thought Paradise Island would be wonderful.

When they arrived on Paradise Island they were disappointed to find that the weather was cold and rainy. To make matters worse, the hotel was still under construction, and the facilities were far from luxurious. They couldn't see the sea from their room but, instead, the view was dominated by ugly factories. When they went down to the beach they found that it was dirty, and that the sea was polluted. They decided to go inland to do some sightseeing instead of spending time on the beach. They were having a good day and Tom posed on a wall while Judy took his picture. Unfortunately he slipped off, fell badly and broke his leg. He had to go to hospital, and his leg was put in plaster. They weren't able to go dancing at all, and Judy spent most of the time writing postcards while Tom gloomily read magazines. Now they are back home again (after some more flight delays) and Tom is on his way to the Travel Agents to complain and to try and get some money back!

Interview

Interviewer: Do you have many complaints about your holidays?

Travel Agent: Certainly not. We check out our hotels and tour operators very carefully.

Interviewer: But obviously in the Tom and Judy case, things went badly wrong.

Travel Agent: Well, they had some bad luck, certainly. But we advise all holidaymakers to take out insurance. We can't be responsible for people doing silly or dangerous things.

Interviewer: And what about the hotel – and the flight delays?

Travel Agent: Paradise Island is a very popular resort and of course there is development all the time. Flights do get delayed at peak times. That's one of the risks of travel.

Interviewer: Are you going to give Tom and Judy any compensation?

Travel Agent: No. We don't take any responsibility for what happened.

16 Olympic success story

Story

Lisa used to race her friends to and from school every day, and when she was fifteen years old she became the National Junior Athletics Champion. She trained very hard every day and was thrilled to gain a place in the team for the Olympics. Then, the day before her race, she had a bad accident. She was hit by a motorcyclist and injured her arm. Most people thought that she would not be able to run, but despite the pain she ran in the 5,000 metres. In a close finish she won the Silver Medal. She received a tremendous welcome when she returned home. Cheering crowds lined the streets and the President gave a grand reception in her honour. Now she is a coach at the National Stadium, but she is also a very popular public figure and makes a lot of money from appearing in advertisements. Lisa is very ambitious and is thinking of becoming a politician. Perhaps one day she will even be President of her country.

Interview

Interviewer: You have seriously injured one of the young stars of the Olympics. How did the accident happen?

Motorcyclist: I was riding through the city centre – quite slowly – when a group of partygoers came out of a hotel. This girl stepped off the pavement without looking. I couldn't avoid her. I'm very sorry about her arm – but there's a lot of damage to my motorbike too. Who's going to pay for that?

Interviewer: Have you seen Lisa since the accident?

Motorcyclist: No. I tried to visit her at the Athletes' Village – but the security people wouldn't let me in. I have sent her some flowers though – and an invitation to dinner – and I hope she does well in the race.

17 Lottery win

Story

Vera and Jack were childhood sweethearts who worked as waitress and cook in the Sunset Café. Things changed overnight when Vera won a prize of a million and a quarter pounds on the Lottery. She got a lot of attention from the press and received hundreds of begging letters from people asking her to help them solve their money problems. She started going to sophisticated cocktail parties and fell for a smooth-talking lady-killer. He was extremely handsome and seemed to be very wealthy. He flirted with her and flattered her. She felt fantastic. She spent a fortune on designer clothes, beauty treatments, and on presents for this man. However, when her new lover left her she was heartbroken. She started to drink more and more alcohol and take anti-depressants. Her so-called friends stopped seeing her. She had nobody. Eventually she went back to see Jack. He was delighted to make a fresh start. With the remains of her Lottery win, Vera bought the café and had it decorated and upgraded. Now they are working together again and share an ambition to make a big success of the "Winning Ticket" Restaurant.

Interview

Interviewer: Jack, how did Vera change when she won all that money?

Jack: She was just overwhelmed by all the publicity and the letters. She couldn't cope with it. She got in with the wrong sort of people and started to spend, spend, spend.

Interviewer: And how did you feel about that?

Jack: It was awful. I knew she was going to be hurt but she cut me out of her life. I didn't see her for ages and there was nothing I could do. That was the worst thing.

Interviewer: And how is she now?

Jack: Well, as you know, she got terribly depressed, but thank goodness she saw sense before it was too late. She's off the pills and things are fine again now.

18 Solo career

Story

The pop group Volcano had a meteoric rise to fame with a string of big hits including the smash hit, *Fire for you*. That is the song they will always be famous for. Following that hit, their wildly energetic stage show was a sell out on their world tour. They performed in cities from New York to Sydney. They were mobbed by screaming fans after each concert, and were totally exhausted and stressed out by the end of that tour. Jake became increasingly dependent on anti-depressants and other drugs. A violent public argument between Belle and Mike attracted a lot of publicity, and soon afterwards the group split up. Tragedy struck a few days later when Jake was found drowned in the swimming pool of his mansion after a party. Dessi and Belle went in search of peace and are now living in a remote cottage. They are guarding their privacy and refusing to give interviews. Mike, on the other hand, has begun a new successful career as a solo artist. His new ballad *Time present* has gone straight into the charts at Number One, as the young fans still idolise him.

Interview

Interviewer:	What do you feel now as you look back at your time with Volcano?
Mike:	A lot of sadness. We were too young to handle so much pressure and we paid, well Jake paid, a terrible price. Nothing can make up for that.
Interviewer:	Dessi and Belle have chosen a very different life style. Do you still see much of them?
Mike:	They don't see much of anyone. I've spoken to Dessi on the phone a couple of times but Belle and I hurt each other pretty badly and I think it'll be a long time before we get together again.
Interviewer:	And your new career? Congratulations on *Time present* making Number One.
Mike:	Thanks. I'm writing music to appeal to a more mature audience these days, so I'm delighted with the response to *Time present*.

19 Endangered species

Story

Since the wars of the 1970s the number of well-armed poachers in Africa has increased and so has the problem of endangered animals. Elephants and rhinos are amongst the most endangered. Poachers shoot elephants and rhinos with automatic weapons, cut off the tusks or horns and leave the bodies to rot. Killing these rare animals except under certain controlled circumstances is illegal. Making and selling things from ivory is also illegal – but the trade continues. Game Wardens try to protect the herds of animals and catch the poachers before they harm the animals. But this is difficult and can be very dangerous. Over a hundred thousand elephants have been killed in Zambia, Central African Republic and Uganda in the past twenty years – and there are very few rhinos left in the wild. These remarkable animals are being slaughtered for their horn, which is regarded as having special powers in traditional Chinese medicine.

In addition to conservation issues, it is in the economic interests of African countries to protect these species because they attract huge income through the tourist industry.

We know about other endangered species such as gorillas, tigers and whales, but in some European countries hunters shoot millions of small birds a year for 'sport'. Surely their attitude is even worse than the rhino poachers, who at least have the excuse that they need money.

Interview

Interviewer: There must be about twenty baby elephants here. How do they come to you?

Kathy: Game wardens from the National parks get in touch if they find orphaned elephants. Usually babies stay very close to the bodies of their parents if the adults have been shot for ivory. They're in great distress, of course, and the young ones can't survive very long in the bush without the protection of adults. They are often sick or starving or injured, and sometimes wounded by bullets. We work with the wardens to arrange transport to get them here as quickly as possible.

Interviewer: And how do you settle them in?

Kathy: Each baby elephant has its own 'foster parent' – a keeper who stays with it twenty-four seven – certainly for the first week or so. It's very touching to see the way the relationship develops.

Interviewer: Do these elephants ever go back to the wild?

Kathy: Yes, always. That's the aim of the scheme. Once they're older they will meet wild elephants and the natural instincts for bonding with the herd will take over.

Interviewer: And I see you have one baby rhino here. What's his story?

Kathy: He's a 'she' actually … her mother was killed by poachers for her horn. We hope that she will go back to the wild one day but it's more difficult. There aren't many rhino, and we have to be very careful – this youngster is growing up here with the baby elephants as companions. She regards them as friends. Of course, the situation would be very different in the National Park – a herd of wild elephant would attack and probably kill a rhino if it got too close – so it will take a lot of planning to reintroduce this rhino to her natural environment.

20 The end of smallpox

Story

Medical Science has conquered smallpox. This terrible disease, which through history has killed millions of people, has now been eradicated.

The breakthrough came in 1796 when a British doctor called Edward Jenner discovered the smallpox vaccine. He injected them with a vaccine which gave them a slight but not very serious form of the disease and enabled their bodies to build up resistance. At first his discovery was treated with suspicion but gradually other countries adopted the technique and by 1900 there was almost no smallpox in Europe or North America but outbreaks of the disease continued in South America, Asia and Africa. They were of epidemic proportions.

In 1965, the World Health Organisation began a vaccination campaign to eradicate smallpox. Teams of doctors have vaccinated millions of people even in remote areas. The last outbreak was in Africa in 1976. However, in case of emergency, huge stores of vaccine are kept in Geneva and New Delhi. But we are still at risk from killer diseases such as the SARS epidemic which began in China, or malaria which in some areas kills thousands of children every day. And of course large parts of the world are still being devastated by the pandemic, AIDS. Medicines are available to help control this disease, but for financial reasons these treatments are mainly available only in developed countries.

Interview

Interviewer:	First of all can I ask you what gives you most satisfaction about your job?
Doctor:	Easy – as a doctor here you can really see that you are making a difference to people's lives. Fifty years ago Polio for example was a major killer. Even when I started it was very common in this part of the world. Now, because of the village vaccination programme, it has almost disappeared completely. Also – I have to be honest – another thing that appeals to me about this work is the sense of adventure. We come by Landrover – or a very small plane – to remote places that hardly anyone has visited. For a few days it's possible to be the honoured guest in a community where the way of life hasn't changed for centuries. It's possible to experience the traditional tribal way of life. That's a real privilege – and it probably won't last for very much longer.
Interviewer:	And is there anything you don't like?
Doctor:	Mosquitoes! But more seriously, a lot of our work now is with AIDS sufferers. We have vaccines which will delay the onset of the disease, but very often by the time we see people it's too late to help. The scale of the problem is devastating. Some villages have lost a whole generation. That's heart breaking.

21 Taking water to the desert

Story

Prince Faisal, a wealthy and powerful politician and businessman, had an imaginative idea for bringing water to the unproductive desert areas of his country. He signed a £100,000,000 contract with a consortium of investors and engineers in Paris to find a suitable iceberg and tow it to the Middle East.

A satellite was used to survey Antarctica and it was decided that the biggest iceberg in the world – measuring 40 by 35 kilometres, and containing 100 million cubic metres of fresh water, would be suitable. The iceberg was tested to make sure it would not crack during the long journey and then it was shaped to make it more streamlined and easier to tow. To do this, holes were drilled into the surface of the iceberg and then explosives were used to blast it into shape. Massive steel ropes were attached to the surface of the iceberg, and a fleet of powerful tugs began to tow it on the 8,000 kilometre journey to its destination. During the course of the eight-month journey the iceberg lost twenty per cent of its bulk. On arrival at its destination, it was sliced into huge blocks.

The blocks were then towed much nearer the shore and the process of melting the ice and pumping the water ashore through a pipeline could begin. From there the fresh water was distributed around the region by pipelines and used to irrigate fields. Now, to the delight of Prince Faisal, there is new life in the desert, a rich harvest of different crops, and jobs in a new agricultural industry.

Interview

Interviewer: Clearly the supply of fresh water is now, and will increasingly be, a major international issue. You've seen the reports of Prince Faisal's project. What's your opinion of it?

Geologist: Rather mixed actually. Of course it's a wonderful thing to irrigate the desert and produce crops; but on balance, I think that this idea has more disadvantages than advantages.

Interviewer: Could you be a bit more specific?

Geologist: Well, everyone is concerned with Global Warming, aren't they? One of the damaging effects of global warming is that the ice cap will melt, sea levels will rise and large areas of the world will be flooded. So it seems to me that anything that damages the ice cap – and blasting icebergs could do that – is a dangerous strategy.

Interviewer: But these icebergs have already broken away from the icecap. The blasting is just to shape them for easier towing. All the water that would have melted and raised the sea level is now being used on land!

Geologist: Yes. Yes. You're right I suppose, but there are alternatives. We have to cut down on the amount of water we waste, get better at storing and distributing rainwater, improve desalination techniques to turn salty water into fresh, and be very active in discovering new underground sources.

Interviewer: So you are actually very much against using icebergs?

Geologist: It may be necessary one day – but for now we should leave the Polar regions alone!

22 Microchip revolution

Story

In less than one generation the miniature microchip which is the size of a matchstick head, has changed life for all of us. Back in the 1960s computers were very large and extremely expensive. Since then, thanks to the rapid design advance and miniaturisation of microchip technology, computers have become compact, affordable and very powerful. A neat, lightweight laptop today does a far larger job than a massive mainframe of the '60s but at a fraction of the price. Microchips are also an integral part of so many everyday items like watches, calculators and phones, as well as sophisticated equipment like scanners used in hospitals or navigation instruments for aircraft.

Microchips are essential for industry, which now relies heavily on robotics for assembly work in factories. They are extremely common in schools and are used for all kinds of educational purposes. In the home, computers provide the normal method of communication through email, of getting information fast from the Internet, and doing the shopping! Mobile phones now combine the functions of camera, music recording device, alarm clock, diary and address book with independent personal communication. A small computer really.

Has this revolution been entirely beneficial? Computers have replaced work previously done by people. The benefits have not been used to put an end to poverty and disease. Perhaps a new generation is growing up addicted to an electronic 'virtual world'?

What is your opinion of the 'Microchip Revolution'?

Interview

Interviewer: Mr Ludd. You've written to the paper saying you want a ban on using electronic devices on trains. That seems very extreme – why are you so upset?

Mr Ludd: I travel to work by train every day –and I hate listening to other people's phone conversations. When you only hear one half of a conversation you can't help trying to guess the rest … and it's impossible not to be distracted.

Interviewer: Perhaps you could buy a pair of ear plugs – or listen to music during the journey?

Mr Ludd: That's another thing I hate. All these people with headsets – they are never properly adjusted. You can always hear the 'thump, thump, thump' of the beat! It drives me up the wall!

Interviewer: And yourself. What do YOU like to do on a train journey?

Mr Ludd: I like to snooze, or read a book. But these days, that's impossible because the person next to me is always taking my space with their laptop or having very loud conversations explaining to someone that they are 'on a train'. I wish these wretched things had never been invented!!!

Interviewer: Do you have any good things to say about the 'micro chip revolution'?

Mr Ludd: Of course I do. I'm not a reactionary! I use computers all the time in my work. But for me, mobile phones in public places are as much of a nuisance as smoking – and we've banned that in most places now, haven't we?

23 Iceland and Cuba

Story

Today we're looking at Iceland, which is situated very far north, almost on the Arctic Circle, and Cuba which is on the Tropic of Cancer and lies between North and South America The islands are roughly the same size in square kilometres, with Cuba much longer and narrower. Iceland has a population of less than a 1/3 million people whereas Cuba is more densely populated, having over 11 million inhabitants. Of the two, Iceland has a much higher income per head. As you would expect from its location, Cuba is hot all the year round with temperatures varying from about twenty-five to thirty-five degrees. It is also rainy, especially from May to November. This contrasts with the climate of Iceland. Temperatures there reach about fifteen degrees in mid-summer, July and August, but are at or below zero for the winter months. The politics of the two countries are very different. Fidel Castro came to power in Cuba in 1953 and turned Cuba into a Marxist State with himself in control. Iceland is a Democratic Republic. Economically both countries have good natural resources. Sugar cane and tobacco are major crops in Cuba. Cuban Rum and Havana cigars are world famous. Tourism is now an important industry. In Iceland visitors come to see the spectacular geysers, but fishing remains the traditional industry.

Interview

Interviewer: Good morning Ambassador. First of all, could you tell me the area of your country?

Ambassador: It's just over 300 thousand square kilometres. Not as big as France or Germany for instance, but considerably bigger than the UK.

Interviewer: Economically, how strong is it?

Ambassador: We are in the Euro zone. There's quite a difference between the North and the South. In general it has one of the stronger economies – certainly stronger than any of the new EU countries like Slovenia or Latvia.

Interviewer: What's the population?

Ambassador: About fifty eight million. That's about the same as the UK.

Interviewer: And the main exports?

Ambassador: The North is industrial and the South mainly agricultural. Not many people know that we are Europe's largest producer of wine.

Interviewer: Could you tell me something about the geography of the country?

Ambassador: Of course. We have a very long coastline and a mountain range running almost the entire length of the country. So that is a big attraction for the millions of visitors. But, I suppose that most of the tourists come to enjoy the atmosphere of the wonderful Renaissance cities like Florence – and to enjoy the best food in the world!!

24 Escape from war-torn country

Story

Today has been a landmark day in Michael's life. He has graduated from college!

People leave their homes and go to different countries for a number of reasons. Often they are economic migrants looking for a better standard of living. In Michael's case the reason was more traumatic. Ten years ago his family was forced out of their war-torn village. Michael and his wife and young child walked three hundred kilometres to the coast to escape the fighting, and in desperation they tried to reach safety by crossing the sea in a small boat. They nearly died of exposure but were rescued by a passing cargo ship. When they reached the nearest country they were treated as stateless people because they had insufficient identity documents. After a long and worrying wait, and a lot of investigation, they were given a visa for Canada. They arrived on a bitterly cold January day and spent the next few months in a tiny room while Michael got a work permit and looked for a job. He worked hard at low-paid, part-time jobs, and at learning the language. Then he began to study at night for the qualifications to enrol for a College course. Ten years after the terrible events, which forced them to leave their home and country, Michael and his family are happily settled into a new life.

Michael's story is fiction, but the situation is recognisable for thousands of people, and things do not always work out so well. There are many difficulties for migrants of all kinds, and for the countries which receive them.

Interview

Interviewer: When did you arrive in Britain? And what were the circumstances of your arrival?

Immigrant: I was one of the so-called 'boat babies'. My parents left Vietnam during the Vietnamese war. I was less than two years old at the time, and after a terrible journey by boat they got to Britain in 1976.

Interviewer: So you don't have any memories of your country of birth?

Immigrant: That's correct in a way, but I grew up in a Vietnamese community in England. So my earliest memories are of very Vietnamese things: cooking smells, language …

Interviewer: And you obviously started school in England.

Immigrant: Yes. By that time the family had moved from the original reception centre on the South coast to join relatives in the Midlands. My father was working in a textile factory. Mum was helping out in a restaurant and doing lots of part time work to make ends meet.

Interviewer: Did you have any trouble learning English?

Immigrant: Well, pronunciation is difficult for Vietnamese speakers, but of course learning from an early age was a big advantage.

Interviewer: Did you start your electronics business straight after school?

Immigrant: Almost. I worked for an uncle who was doing something similar for a couple of years and then started up on my own. I think I was lucky – to be in the right place at the right time!

Interviewer: Do you think of yourself as British or Vietnamese?

Immigrant: Mmmm … British … I hesitated a little because an important part of my life is my Vietnamese background and culture.

Interviewer: And have you ever been back to your country of birth?

Immigrant: I've thought about it, and I keep in touch with some distant relatives I've never seen. It would be possible now but … my life is here and I'm happy to keep it like that.

Answer key

1 Another day, another dollar page 7
2 1 breakfast 2 servants; suit 3 chauffeur
4 meetings 5 sales reports 6 entertains
7 two o'clock 8 exhausted 9 same
4 1c 2h 3f 4b 5a 6g 7e 8d
5 1 Yes, he does.
2 Yes, he does.
3 No, she doesn't.

2 Environmental disaster page 9
2 1f 2g 3i 4a 5j 6h 7e 8b 9d 10l 11c 12k
4 1e 2c 3j 4g 5f 6i 7h 8a 9b 10d
5 1 Yes, they did. 2 Yes, he does. 3 They can't make a
living because they haven't got a boat.

3 Gap year page 11
2 1 country = world 2 dolphins = sharks
3 sausages = pasta 4 clothes = money
5 inside = outside 6 trains = photos
7 trees = mountains 8 plane = boat
9 walked = cycled 10 zoo = carnival
11 worked = danced 12 friends = parents
4 1 climbed – b 2 arrived – f 3 ate – e 4 cycled – h
5 swam – a 6 visited – g 7 bought – c 8 danced – d
5 1 He set off an alarm and got to Francis as soon as
possible.
2 He thinks he's stupid.

4 UFO story page 13
2 1d 2h 3a 4j 5b 6l 7c 8e 9f 10g 11i 12k
4 1b 2d 3h 4a 5c 6g 7e 8f
5 1 No, she doesn't. 2 She thinks he must have hit his
head.

5 Football crazy page 15
2 1 match 2 stadium 3 players; pitch 4 crowd
5 foul; referee 6 penalty 7 won 8 kitchen
9 highlights
4 1e 2b 3d 4a 5i 6g 7c 8f 9h
5 1 No, he isn't. 2 He's going to drink some beer and
then go to a club.

6 Mother Teresa page 17
2 1g 2d 3f 4e 5c 6b 7a
4 1d 2e 3f 4c 5a 6b 7g
5 1 It flies doctors and nurses to remote areas.
2 People donate money and they publish a magazine
and videos to show people what they are doing.

7 Dinner disaster page 19
2 1 invited 2 prepared 3 laid; candles 4 dress 5 arrived
6 horrified; empty 7 burst; rushed 8 fish and chip
9 cat

4 1 Mr Plummer 2 Mrs Smith 3 Mrs Smith 4 Mr Smith
5 Mr Smith 6 Mr or Mrs Smith 7 Mr or Mrs Plummer
8 Mrs Smith 9 Mr or Mrs Plummer 10 The cat
5 1 No, Mr Plummer is Mr Smith's boss. 2 Dave and
Isobel 3 Yes. The Plummers have invited the Smiths
for dinner in two weeks' time.

8 Fashion fads page 21
2 1 trousers = dresses 2 shorts = jackets
3 cheap = expensive 4 pyjamas = uniforms
5 long = mini 6 shoes = jeans
7 swimming = baseball
4 2 7 – today
3 6 –1970s
4 2 – Victorian/1880s
5 6 – 1970s
6 5 – 1960s
7 3 – 1920s
8 4 – 1940s/wartime
9 5 -- 1960s
10 7 -- today
5 1 She likes the publicity and the money.
2 She usually wears casual clothes. 3 Because the
interviewer asks her about her private life.

9 High noon page 23
2 1f 2c 3d 4h 5g 6a 7b 8e
4 1 He has a big, black moustache. He looks mean and
aggressive.
2 They ran away.
3 He went to the saloon bar.
4 He went at 12 o'clock – high noon.
6 He hid.
7 Student's own answers
5 1 He wanted to help his cousin, Hank.
2 The Sheriff let Hank go.

10 Fitness for ever! page 25
2 1 mirror, overweight 2 exercise 3 laughed 4 talking
5 tripped 6 bit 7 rain 8 backache; threw
4 1 b 2d 3e 4a 5c
5 1 She runs to the Centre, she uses the cycles and the
rowing machines. She does some weight training. She
swims forty lengths. She cycles to work. She goes to a
Jazz Dance class. She does aerobics.
2 She was very ill three years ago and had to start
exercising to build up her strength.

11 Bank robbers on camera page 27
2 1 customers 2 camera 3 witnesses 4 robbers
5 informer 6 girlfriends 7 arrested 8 gunpoint
4 1 bulletin 2 villa 3 cashier 4 witnesses
5 statement 6 criminals

5 1 In a night club on a Greek island.   2 He said he was a dentist.   3 No, she didn't.

12 Carry on camping page 29
2 1g 2e 3a 4f 5h 6b 7c 8d
4 1 disagree   2 standing still   3 put up a tent
4 no petrol   5 cow   6 fence   7 collapsed
5 1 Finding that his wife and the car were not there in the morning.
2 All their clothes were wet and muddy and it took her three days to clean them all.
3 Mr Thompson wants to go camping again but Mrs Thompson wants to go to Spain.

13 Earthquake hits city page 31
2 1 shake 2 trapped 3 Rescuers 4 news 5 medicine
6 raise 7 black market 8 rebuilding 9 buildings; tents
4 1c 2a 3f 4h 5d 6g 7b 8e 9i
5 1 By selling aid to Kanahz on the black market.
2 Only 25% of the aid reached the disaster area.
3 No.

14 Treasure restored page 33
2 1 potter   2 wealthy   3 vineyard   4 undamaged
5 merchant   6 ship   7 wrecked   8 divers
9 restorer   10 auction   1 museum
4 1b 2g 3d 4f 5a 6e 7c
5 1 No, she isn't.
2 The Egyptian mummies.

15 A week in paradise page 35
2 1 perfect 2 wedding 3 plane 4 disappointed
5 factories 6 polluted 7 posed 8 slipped
9 plaster 10 postcards 11 gloomily 12 complain
4 1 luxury 2 inland 4 gloomily 5 pose 6 delayed
5 1 No. 2 No.

16 Olympic success story page 37
2 1k 2i 3c 4g 5b 6d 7e 8a 9j 10h 11f 12l
4 1 coach 2 champion 3 injure 4 cheer
5 reception
5 1 It was Lisa's fault. 2 No, he hasn't.

17 Lottery win page 39
2 1 sweethearts 2 overnight 3 press   4 begging
5 handsome   6 flirted 7 treatments
8 heartbroken   9 alcohol   10 delighted
11 decorated   12 together
4 1 begging 2 flatter 3 ambition 5 sweethearts
6 fortune
5 1 No, he didn't.   2 Yes, she has.

18 Solo career page 41
2 1 mountain = pop group   2 angry = famous
3 holiday = tour   4 danced = performed
5 whispering = screaming   6 lively = exhausted

7 photos = drugs 8 hug = argument
9 disappeared = split up   10 toilet = swimming pool
11 noise = peace   12 useless = successful
4 1 mobbed   2 split up   3 idolise   4 tragedy
5 exhausted   6 sell out
5 1 He feels sad.   2 He has spoken to Dessi but he hasn't been in touch with Belle.

19 Endangered species page 43
2 1b 2g 3d 4c 5e 6f 7a
4 1 to slaughter   2 illegal   3 to rot   4 ivory   5 a herd
6 automatic weapons
5 1 Orphaned elephants   2 They go back to the wild.
3 More difficult.

20 The end of smallpox page 45
2 1 conquered   2 eradicated   3 vaccine   4 injected
5 outbreaks   6 campaign   7 remote   8 emergency   9 risk
4 1 disease   2 outbreak   3 finds   5 can't   6 work
5 1 He can see that he can make a difference to the people's lives.   2 Mosquitoes and the fact that he is often too late to help people with AIDS.

21 Taking water to the desert page 47
2 1 imaginative   2 consortium   3 satellite   4 suitable
5 crack   6 surface   7 blast   8 tugs   9 bulk
10 destination   11 melting   12 irrigate
3 1 irrigate   2 massive   3 consortium   4 tug   5 blast
6 melt
5 1 He is against the idea.   2 Cut down on how much water we waste; get better at storing and distributing rain water; improve desalination techniques; look for new underground sources of water.

22 Microchip revolution page 49
2 (& 4) 1c (c) 2f (d) 3a (e) 4e (a) 5d (f) 6b (b)
5 1 People talking on mobile phones on trains.
2 No, he uses computers all the time in his work.
3 Student's own answer

23 Iceland and Cuba page 51
2 1 situated   2 size 3 climate   4 politics
5 resources   6 Tourism
4 1T 2F 3F   4T   5T 6F 7F 8T 9T 10T
5 1 Italy   2 It has one of the stronger economies in the world.   3 The mountain range and coastline, the Renaissance cities and the best food in the world.

24 Escape from war-torn country page 53
2 1 graduated   2 village   3 escape   4 safety   5 cargo
boat 6 identity   7 visa   8 January   9 bitterly
10 permit   11 low-paid   12 settled
4 1b 2e 3d 4c 5a
5 1 1976   2 He has an electronics business.   3 His Vietnamese background and culture are important to him but his life is in Britain.

Material written by: Mark Fletcher and Richard Munns

Commissioning Editor: Jacquie Bloese

Editor: Viv Lambert

Cover design: Eddie Rego

Designer: Janet McCallum

Illustrators: David Farris, Pete Smith (Beehive Illustration), Magic Eye (Beehive Illustration)

Cover artwork: David Farris

Mary Glasgow Magazines (Scholastic Ltd.)
Euston House
24 Eversholt Street
London NW1 1DB

Printed in the UK.